YOUR RETIREMENT PLANNING PLAYBOOK

Your Retirement Coach, Joe Hamel

This book discusses general concepts for retirement planning, and is not intended to provide tax or legal advice. Individuals are urged to consult with their tax and legal professionals regarding these issues. It is important to know a) that annuities and some of their features have costs associated with them; b) that annuities used to fund IRAs do not afford any additional measure of tax deferral for the IRA owner; c) that income received from annuities and securities may be taxable; and d) that securities' past performance does not influence or predict future results.

Printed in the United States of America

First Printing, 2016

Gradient Positioning Systems, LLC
4105 Lexington Avenue North, Suite 110
Arden Hills, MN 55126
(877) 901-0894

Contributors: Nick Stovall, Mike Binger, Nate Lucius and Gradient Positioning Systems, LLC.

Gradient Positioning Systems, LLC and Joe Hamel are not affiliated with or endorsed by the Social Security Administration or any government agency.

TABLE OF CONTENTS

INTRODUCTION

Bill's father worked at the steel manufacturing plant in Cleveland, Ohio. When he retired, the pension fund he had contributed to his entire life went belly up, and Bill's father had to retire with a much smaller pension than he deserved.

Now that Bill and his wife are nearing their retirement, it seems they are up against even more uncertainty. Is the next major market correction just around the corner? Can they count on their Social Security benefits? How will they afford health care if one of them becomes chronically ill? Bill knows he needs to get some advice about how to better position their assets for retirement, but who should he listen to, and where can he go for advice that he can he trust?

Retirement is a time in your life when many decisions have to be made: decisions about how to best optimize your Social Security benefit and pension options, choose your Medicare plans, solve the income gap, protect yourself and your spouse in the event of a long-term care situation, get your legal documents in order—and don't forget your investment decisions, exposure to risk and opportunity for returns. *These decisions generally have to be made in a short time frame, yet they go on to affect your income and the quality of your life for years to come.*

You only get to retire once, and you've never retired before, so how do you know how to make decisions that will result in the best possible outcome for you? In short, how do you get it right the first time?

As an Investment Advisor Representative with more than 16 years of experience in the financial and insurance industry, I may not have retired before, but I have coached hundreds of retirees through the process. I've also spent the last 10 years coaching my three sons in youth sports, and this year I'm finding out how to coach an all-girls team as I work with my daughter's basketball team. What I've found is that the same principles that lead to championships on the field or court can also help you win in the game of retirement.

People learn best by doing. That's why this retirement book is designed to take you through the plays so you can approach retirement better informed, better educated and with all the moves you need to take the ball and run.

WHAT YOU HEAR FROM BOTH SIDES OF THE FENCE

Part of the reason it's gotten more difficult for retirees today has to do with all the noise out there about what you should and should not be doing with your retirement savings. Since the year 2000, we've had two major market corrections and a Ponzi investment scandal known in the news headlines as "the scam of the century." Many people like Bill in our story above who are entering or planning for retirement saw their account balances go down anywhere between 40 to 60 percent during these recent market corrections, and they have spent the last several years trying to recover. That has left many people wondering, when will the next downturn come?

For investors who choose to take a "do-it-yourself approach", there is no lack of information on the Internet. While information can be a good thing, too much can lead to overload, especially when there are bloggers and websites and surveys that contradict each other. One financial website will tell you that the stock market is the absolute best place to be; the very next article will tell you the exact opposite. When you hear it from both sides of the fence, it's very difficult for the average investor to make sense of what's relevant to their situation. Like the kid on the pitcher's mound being yelled at by mom, dad and their teammates and coaches, there's a lot of noise!

Your retirement coach is the voice of reason who can help you cut through all the advice that doesn't pertain to you. Many retirees step on to the playing field of retirement exposed to far more risk than they realize. If you have no plan and no guarantees in place for the retirement income that you need, you end up relying on outdated advice that no longer applies in today's volatile, global economy. Just taking regular 5-percent withdrawals from your IRA might seem like a good idea, until that account goes down by 30 or 40 percent, and then you have to increase the percentage of your withdrawal just to make ends meet. That's a real concern, because taking out a regular percentage on an asset that's going down in value is a recipe for running out of money before you run out of life!

HOW THE GAME HAS CHANGED

If following outdated advice can get you into trouble when it comes to securing income, then it is possible that doing what you have always done can get you into even more trouble. Why? *During retirement, the rules of the investing game change.*

Your working years are what I call *the accumulation years* of your investing life. In your 20s, 30s, 40s and even on into your 50s, you are drawing a regular paycheck. That paycheck allows you to contribute to a 401k or retirement plan. When you are in that phase, it actually benefits you more if the stock market is low, because that's what allows you to buy more shares with the same amount of money. It's like getting shares of stock on sale. As the stock market increases in value, as it historically does, you will have more shares and a nice, fat 401(k), which is exactly what you want. Once you can see retirement on your time horizon, all that changes.

Retirement is what I call *the income phase* or *the distribution phase* of your investing life. Instead of earning a paycheck and adding dollars to your account, you are taking those dollars out. It's time to sell those investments you got on sale to earn the profit that shows up on your account balance. The problem is, if the market drops, you aren't going to get that profit. You are no longer contributing to your account, and that loss matters more.

When you realize how imperative this money is to the security of your retirement income, you start to develop a different mindset when it comes to risk. **Going from *the accumulation phase* into *the distribution phase* means that you want to protect and preserve everything you can in order to provide the income that you have rightfully earned.** Taking a loss now, just prior to or shortly after retiring, can be the equivalent of getting your pension cut in half. After working and saving for an entire lifetime, nobody deserves that.

HOW TO FIND YOUR SWEET SPOT

In baseball, your sweet spot is the place on the bat where it is most effective to hit the ball. When you hit your sweet spot, the ball is hit hard and goes as far as it possibly can. This can be compared to making the dollars in your portfolio go as far as they possibly can.

While it certainly helps to have a lot of money to work with, the reality is that unless you get an inheritance or win the lottery, the amount of your nest egg is what you have to work with. Whether you retire with $250,000 or with $1 million, what you have is what you have. That's why it's extremely important to find your metaphorical "sweet spot" when designing your retirement plan. When all the decisions you make concerning your investments, taxes and funding your long-term care needs all work together, then you've found the sweet spot that allows you to do the absolute most with what you have. That is the efficiency a good plan can deliver.

As your retirement coach, designing the plays to find your sweet spot is a process that goes something like this:

> » **Line Up Your Defenses:** Most people step up to the retirement plate metaphorically "swinging for the fences", still trying to hit those big returns. While accumulation is an important part of most retirement plans, you don't want to run the risk of striking out on day one. Chapter 1 introduces you to the "Rule of 100" and the concepts of what I call "Hope So" and "Know So" money so you can get a better understanding of the risk in your portfolio. We'll run you through several risk exercises in Chapter 2, and look at your portfolio using the Color of Money concept so you can start organizing your assets to run plays that will score you income.

> » **Create An Income Strategy:** Anyone who spends time on the ball field will hear a coach yelling the old adage, "Keep your eye on the ball!" During retirement, that ball is the equivalent of your income. In so many ways, the ability of your investments to supply you with lifetime income is the only thing that matters. It leads to all other successes. Chapter 3 takes a look at income planning, and

addresses what happens to your income should one spouse pass away. Loss of income due to spousal death can result in your partner having to endure unnecessary financial hardship. You can help prevent that situation with a few well-designed plays.

» **Your Star Player—Social Security:** Most people will look to their Social Security benefit as a first source of guaranteed income. This is a benefit that you have paid into your entire life, and when structured properly, it can help free up more of your assets for other needs. Chapter 4 takes you through the drills of roll-up options and filing strategies that can help increase the amount of your Social Security benefit, providing you with a higher lifetime income.

» **Create Your Own Pension Plan:** If you are retiring without a traditional pension, you may find your Social Security benefit will not be enough to satisfy your income needs. This is where the assets you have so carefully saved come into play. You want to secure the portion of your assets required for income and turn those savings into a reliable income stream. Chapter 5 talks about today's new hybrid annuities that allow you to participate in market-linked gains without risk of market loss.

» **The Retirement Red Zone:** Once your income needs have been met, it's time to look at the accumulation plays that can keep you in the game. The five years before retirement and the five years after can have significant impacts on your overall financial position in retirement. Chapter 6 shows you why suffering a large loss during that window can negatively affect your lifestyle, and eventually take you out of the retirement game altogether. Chapter 7 looks at the advantages of managed "Yellow Money" as one way to help you pass through this red zone more comfortably.

» **The Secret To Long-term Care Planning:** The more I go out into the field with my clients who are starting to advance in age, the more it becomes apparent that incorporating an element of long-term care planning is vital to the stability of every retirement plan. There are several strategies to use when preparing for this type of unforeseen event, and not all of them cost money. Chapter 12 takes you through what you need to know to protect and preserve your assets, including the secret sauce to long-term care planning using the little-known ingredients of hybrid insurance options to protect yourself and the ones you love.

A WINNING TRADITION

As a regular runner, I've noticed that when I have my attention focused on the ground, watching my every step, my run feels longer, more stressful, and I tire more easily. On the other hand, when I have my head up, looking at the terrain ahead, the run goes easier and I enjoy myself more. I still occasionally glance down to get my bearings, but my focus is on my goal and the scenery along the way instead of all the steps I have to take to get there.

The process of planning for retirement can feel a bit like running a long distance. When you look at all the issues (income planning, Social Security maximization, estate planning, long-term care planning) it can feel like watching your feet go up a really steep hill. That's no way to start what should be a rewarding phase of life.

My job as a retirement coach is to help you enjoy the process, with your head held high and the end goal in mind. My firm is committed to a planning process that takes things one step at a time. In order to design a plan that can handle the brunt of unforeseen tackles and the risk at play in today's economy, I have created strategic affiliations with professionals in all areas of retirement planning, including the addition of an elder law attorney. This multidisciplinary approach gives you access to private third-partner money managers, Certified Public Accountants (CPAs) and estate planning attorneys to help you create the most solid defense possible.

As a financial professional who specializes in income planning and the challenges specific to retirement, nothing satisfies me more than knowing my clients have a sense of calm and confidence about their income, investments, their legacy goals and their health. Knowing you have a solid plan in play is what ultimately leads to a worry-free retirement, so you can spend your time worrying about the important things, such as where you will take you next trip, and how best to spoil the grandkids. When I hear people talking about their trips and their grandkids, that's when I feel I've really done my job, and that's what I want for you: a winning retirement that gives you the peace of mind you deserve.

– *Joe Hamel*, Your Retirement Coach

1
GAME ON:
ORGANIZING YOUR ASSETS

Will we have enough money for retirement?

Will your Social Security benefit, savings and other retirement assets be enough? If you're like Raymond and Diane, you hope so. When the couple turned 60 years old, they started thinking about what their lives would be like in the next 10 years. When would they retire? What would their retirement look like? How much money did they have?

They could both count on Social Security benefits, but neither one really knew how much their monthly checks would be, or when to file for them. Raymond had a modest pension that he could begin collecting at age 67. He had always hoped to retire before that age. Diane had a 401(k), but she honestly wasn't exactly sure how it worked, how she could draw money from it and how much income it would provide once she retired.

While Raymond and Diane may sound like they're totally in the dark about their retirement, the truth is there are a lot of people just like them. They know retirement is coming and know they have some assets to rely on, but they aren't sure how it will all come together to provide them with a retirement income.

You spend your entire working life hoping what you put into your retirement accounts will help you live comfortably once you clock out of the workforce for good. The key word in that sentiment and the word that can make retirement feel like a looming problem instead of a rewarding life stage, is *hope*. You hope you'll have enough money.

Leaving your retirement up to chance is unadvisable by nearly any standard, yet millions of people find themselves *hoping* instead of planning for a happy ending. While you may have built up a 401(k), an IRA, and Social Security benefits, do you know what your financial picture really looks like?

Money represents more than the paper it's printed on. It is the embodiment of your time, your talents, and your commitments. It buys the food you eat, the house you sleep in, the car you drive, and the clothes you wear. It also helps provide you with the lifestyle you want to live once you retire.

You have spent a lifetime earning it, spending it, and hopefully, accumulating it. When the time comes for retirement, you want your money to provide you with a comfortable lifestyle and stable income after your working days are done. You might also have other desires, such as traveling, purchasing property, or moving to be closer to your family (or farther away). You may also want your assets to provide for your loved ones after you are gone.

The truth is that it takes more than just money to fulfill those needs and desires. Your income, your plans for retirement, your future healthcare expenses, and the continued accumulation of your assets after you stop working and drawing a paycheck all rely on one thing: *You*.

VISUALIZE YOUR RETIREMENT

The responsibility of investing and planning for retirement is a heavy burden to shoulder and it can be difficult to know what move to make first. Athletes sometimes feel this same kind of pressure when out on the court or on the field knowing all eyes are on them during a particularly stressful moment. One of the best ways to prepare for the stress of the big game and for retirement is to tap into the benefits of visualization.

Many coaches today instruct their athletes on how to not just physically run plays, but how to visualize them on the inner screen of their mind. Studies have shown that this kind of practice can be just as effective as actual court or field time. Visualization is especially effective when done at night, just before bed. With eyes closed, you can imagine yourself at the free-throw line of a basketball court, hearing the roar of the crowd and teammates screaming and coach yelling; you smell the gym, see the net and feel the ball go off your fingertips and swish into the basket. For baseball players, your picture might include the smell of the grass and the heat of a summer night; you see that pitcher looking at you and that ball coming in, then you hear the crack of the bat and see the baseball as it goes right up center field for a base hit. How does it feel when your teammates mob you and pat your helmet, and in the stands when your fans are on their feet going wild with applause after you delivered the winning hit?

It feels pretty great, and that's just the way you want your retirement to feel.

What do you want your retirement to look like? This is a big picture question designed to get you thinking about the long term. Choosing the best investment solutions for your retirement begins with an examination of the kinds of things you see yourself doing during retirement and the people who you will be doing those things with. Your financial professional will need to know what's important to you first before he or she can design the plays to help you get what you want.

What do you see yourself doing in retirement? Are you and your spouse hanging out on the beach? Driving around in a nice motor home? Visiting kids and grandkids? Out on the town? Or are you at home enjoying your T.V. shows? Taking a pottery class? On the golf course?

The way you approach your retirement impacts your income, the taxes your assets are subject to, your financial stability in the future, and your legacy. It is a truism among financial professionals that *one hour of planning can be worth more than an entire lifetime of working and saving* when it comes to retirement.

How is that possible? The fact of the matter is that after working and saving for a lifetime, entering retirement changes all of the rules you have known and followed for your entire career. Making sure your assets last for your lifetime will depend on how you decide to invest them, and in what order you will spend them. With forces like inflation, market volatility, and fluctuating interest rates working against you, knowing what to do with your assets has never been more important. And the difference between making a good decisions and a bad decision has never had such a dramatic impact on how people retire.

The question isn't CAN you or SHOULD you put your money to work for you and your family. It's HOW.

KEEPING IT REAL

Advice about what to do with money has been around as long as money has existed. Hindsight allows us to see which advice was good and which advice didn't cut the mustard. Some sources of advice have been around for a very long time. While there are some basic investment concepts that have stood the test of time, most strategies that work adapt to changing conditions in the market, in the economy and the world, as well as changes in your personal circumstances.

The reality is that investment strategies and savings plans that worked in the past have encountered challenging new circumstances that have turned them on their heads. The Great Recession of the early 2000's highlighted how old investment ideas were not only ineffective but incredibly destructive to the retirement plans of millions of Americans. The dawn of an entirely restructured health care system brings with it new options and challenges that will undoubtedly change the way insurance companies provide investment products and services.

Perhaps the most important lessons investors learned from the Great Recession is that not understanding where your money is invested (and the potential risks of those investments) can work against you, your plans for retirement and your legacy. Saving and investing money isn't enough to truly get the most out of it. You must have a planful approach to managing your assets.

Essentially, managing your money and your investments is an ongoing process that requires customization and adaptation to a changing world. And make no mistake; the world is always changing. What worked for your parents or even your parents' parents was probably good advice back then. People in retirement or approaching retirement today need new ideas and professional guidance.

HOPE SO VS. KNOW SO MONEY

Let's take a look at some of the basic truths about money as it relates to saving for retirement.

There are essentially two kinds of money: *Hope So* and *Know So*. Everyone can divide their money into these two categories. Some have more of one kind than the other. The goal isn't to eliminate one kind of money but to balance them as you approach retirement.

Hope So Money is money that is at risk. It fluctuates with the market. It has no minimum guarantee. It is subject to investor activity, stock prices, market trends, buying trends, etc. You get the picture. This money is exposed to more risk but also has the potential for more reward. Because the market is subject to change, you can't really be sure what the value of your investments will be worth in the future. You can't really *rely* on it at all. For this reason, we refer to it as Hope So Money. This doesn't mean you shouldn't have some money invested in the market, but it would

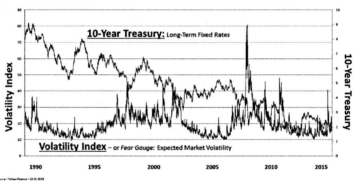

The VIX, or volatility index, of the market represents expected market volatility. When the VIX Drops, economic experts expect less volatility. When the VIX rises, more volatility is expected.

1. VIX is a trademarked ticker symbol for the Chicago Board Options Exchange (CBOE) Market Volatility Index, a popular measure of the implied volatility of S&P 500 index options. Often referred to as the fear index or the fear gauge, it represents one measure of the market's expectation of stock market volatility over the next 30 day period. (wikipedia.com)

2. The CBOE 10-Year Treasury note (TNX) is based on 10 times the yield-to-maturity on the most recently auctioned 10-year Treasury note.

be dangerous to assume you can know what it will be worth in the future.

Hope So Money is an important element of a retirement plan, especially in the early stages of planning when you can trade volatility for potential returns, and when a longer investment timeframe is available to you. In the long run, time can smooth out the ups and downs of money exposed to the market. Working with a professional and leveraging a long-term investment strategy has the potential to create rewarding returns from Hope So Money.

Know So Money, on the other hand, is safer when compared to Hope So Money. Know So Money is made up of dependable, low-risk or no-risk money, and investments that you can count on. Social Security is one of the most common forms of Know So Money. Income you draw or will draw from Social Security is guaranteed. You have paid into Social Security your entire career, and you can rely on that money during your retirement. Unlike the market, rates of growth for Know So Money are dependent on 10-year treasury rates. The 10-year treasury, or TNX, is commonly considered to represent a very secure and safe place for your money, hence Know So Money. The 10-year treasury drives key rates for things such as mortgage rates or CD rates. Know So Money may not be as exciting as Hope So Money, but it is safer. You can safely be fairly sure you will have it in the future.

Knowing the difference between Hope So and Know So Money is an important step towards a successful retirement plan. People who are 55 or older and who are looking ahead to retirement should be relying on more Know So Money than Hope So Money.

Ideally, the rates of return on Hope So and Know So Money would have an overlapping area that provided an acceptable rate of risk for both types of money. In the early 1990s, interest rates were high and market volatility was low. At that time, you could invest in either Hope So or Know So Money options because the rates of return were similar from both Know So and Hope So investments, and you were likely to be fairly successful with a wide range of investment options. At that time, you could expose yourself to an acceptable amount of risk or an acceptable fixed rate. Basically, it was difficult to make a mistake during that time period. Today, you don't have those options. Market volatility is at all-time highs while interest rates are at all-time lows. They are so far apart from each other that it is hard to know what to do with your money.

Yesterday's investment rules may not work today. Not only could they hamper achieving your goals, they may actually harm your financial situation. We are currently in a period when the rates for Know So Money options are at historic lows, and the volatility of Hope So Money is higher than ever. There is no overlapping acceptable rate, making both options less than ideal. *Because of this uncertain financial landscape, wise investment strategies are more important now than ever.*

This unique situation requires fresh ideas and investment tools that haven't been relied on in the past. Investing the way your parents did will not pay off. The majority of investment ideas used by financial professionals in the 1990s aren't applicable to today's markets. That kind of investing will likely get you in trouble and compromise your retirement. Today, you need a better PLAN.

HOW MUCH RISK ARE YOU EXPOSED TO?

Many investors don't know how much risk they are exposed to. It is helpful to organize your assets so you can have a clear understanding of how much of your money is at risk and how much is in safer holdings. This process starts with listing all your assets.

Let's take a look at the two kinds of money:

Hope So Money is, as the name indicates, money that you *hope* will be there when you need it. Hope So Money represents what you would like to get out of your investments. Examples of Hope So Money include:
- Stock market funds, including index funds
- Mutual funds
- Variable annuities
- REITS

Know So Money is money that you know you can count on. It is safer money that isn't exposed to the level of volatility as the asset types noted above. You can more confidently count on having this money when you need it. Examples of Know So Money are:
- Government backed bonds
- Savings and checking accounts
- Fixed income annuities
- CDs
- Treasuries
- Money market accounts

> » *John had a modest brokerage account that he added to when he could. When he changed jobs a couple years ago, at age 58, John transferred his 401(k) assets into an IRA. Just a few years from retirement, he is now beginning to realize that nearly every dollar he has saved for retirement is subject to market risk.*
>
> *Intuitively, he knows that the time has come to shift some assets to an alternative that is safer, but how much is the right amount?*

THE RULE OF 100

Determining the amount of risk that is right for you is dependent on a number of variables. You need to feel comfortable with where and how you are investing your money, and your financial professional is obligated to help you make decisions that put your money in places that fit your risk criteria.

Your retirement needs to first accommodate your day-to-day income needs. How much money do you need to maintain your lifestyle? When do you need it?

Managing your risk by having a balance of Hope So Money vs. Know So Money is a good start that will put you ahead of the curve. But how much Know So Money is enough to secure your income needs during retirement, and how much Hope So Money is enough to allow you to continue to benefit from an improving market?

In short, how do you begin to know how much risk you should be exposed to?

While there is no single approach to investment risk determination advice that is universally applicable to everyone, there are some helpful guidelines. One of the most useful is called *The Rule of 100*.

The average investor needs to accumulate assets to create a retirement plan that provides income during retirement and also allows for legacy planning. To accomplish this, they need to balance the amount of risk to which they are exposed. Risk is required because, while Know So Money is safer, more reliable and more dependable, it doesn't grow very fast, if at all. Today's historically low interest rates barely break even with current inflation. Hope So Money, while less dependable, has more potential for growth. Hope So Money can eventually become Know So Money once you move it to an investment with lower risk. Everyone's risk diversification will be different depending on their goals, age and their existing assets.

So how do you decide how much risk your assets should be exposed to? Where do you begin? Luckily, there's a guideline you can use to start making decisions about risk management. It's called the Rule of 100.

YOUR BALL: APPLYING THE RULE

The Rule of 100 is a general rule that helps shape asset diversification* for the average investor. The rule states that the number 100 minus an investor's age equals the amount of assets they should have exposed to risk.

> **The Rule of 100**: 100 - (your age) = the percentage of your assets that should be exposed to risk (Hope So Money).

For example, if you are a 30-year-old investor, the Rule of 100 would indicate that you should be focusing on investing primarily in the market and taking on a substantial amount of risk in your portfolio. The Rule of 100 suggests that 70 percent of your investments should be exposed to risk.

$$100 - (30 \text{ years of age}) = 70 \text{ percent}$$

Now, not every 30-year-old should have exactly 70 percent of their assets in mutual funds and stocks. The Rule of 100 is based on

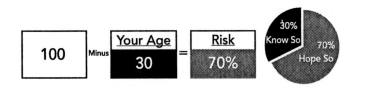

* *Asset Diversification disclosure – Diversification and asset allocation does not assure of or guarantee better performance and cannot eliminate the risk of investment loss. Before investing, you should carefully read the applicable volatility disclosure for each of the underlying funds, which can be found in the current prospectus.*

your chronological age, not your "financial age," which could vary based on your investment experience, your aversion or acceptance of risk and other factors. While this rule isn't an ironclad solution to anyone's finances, it's a pretty good place to start. Once you've taken the time to look at your assets with a professional to determine your risk exposure, you can use the Rule of 100 to make changes that put you in a more stable investment position—one that reflects your comfort level.

Perhaps when you were age 30 and starting your career, like in the example above, it made sense to have 70 percent of your money in the market: you had time on your side. You had plenty of time to save more money, work more and recover from a downturn in the market. Retirement was ages away, and your earning power was increasing. And indeed, younger investors should take on more risk for exactly those reasons. The potential reward of long-term involvement in the market outweighs the risk of investing when you are young.

Risk tolerance generally reduces as you get older, however. If you are 40 years old and lose 30 percent of your portfolio in a market downturn this year, you have 20 or 30 years to recover it. If you are 68 years old, you have five to 10 years (or less) to make the same recovery. That new circumstance changes your whole retirement perspective. At age 68, it's likely that you simply aren't as interested in suffering through a tough stock market. There is less time to recover from downturns, and the stakes are higher. The money you have saved is money you will soon need to provide you with income, or is money that you already need to meet your income demands.

Much of the flexibility that comes with investing earlier in life is related to *compounding*. Compounded earnings can be incredibly powerful over time. The longer your money has time to compound, the greater your wealth will be. This is what most people talk about when they refer to putting their money to work. This is also why the Rule of 100 favors risk for the young. If you start investing when you are young, you can invest smaller amounts of money in a more aggressive fashion because you have the potential to make a profit in a rising market and you can harness the power of compounding earnings. When you are 40, 50 or 60 years old, that potential becomes less and less and you are forced to have more money at lower amounts of risk to realize the same returns. **It basically becomes more expensive to prudently invest the older you get.**

You risk not having a recovery period the older you get, so you should have less of your assets at risk in volatile investments. You should shift with the Rule of 100 to protect your assets and ensure that they will provide you with the income you need in retirement. Let's look at another example that illustrates how the Rule of 100 becomes more critical as you age. An 80-year-old investor who is retired and is relying on retirement assets for income, for example, needs to depend on a solid amount of Know So Money. The Rule of 100 says an 80-year-old investor should have a maximum of 20 percent of his or her assets at risk. Depending on the investor's financial position, even less risk exposure may be required. *You are the only person who can make this kind of determination*, but the Rule of 100 can help. Everyone has their own level of comfort. Your Rule of 100 results will be based on your values and attitudes as well as your comfort with risk.

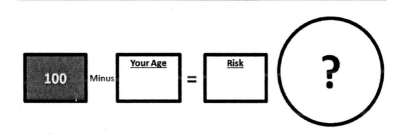

The Rule of 100 can apply to overarching financial management and to specific investment products that you own as well. Take the 401(k) for example. Many people have them, but not many people understand how their money is allocated within their 401(k). An employer may have someone who comes in once a year and explains the models and options that employees can choose from, but that's as much guidance as most 401(k) holders get. Many 401(k) options include target date funds that change their risk exposure over time, essentially following a form of the Rule of 100. Selecting one of these options can often be a good move for employees because they shift your risk as you age, securing more Know So Money when you need it. A financial professional can look at your assets with you and discuss alternatives to optimize your balance between Know So and Hope So Money.

CHAPTER 1 RECAP //

- Planning for a successful retirement begins with visualizing what you want your retirement to look like. The kinds of things you want to be doing and the people who you will be doing those things with are what shape your investments choices and decisions.
- The rules for retirement planning have changed. Investing the way your parents did may not pay off and the majority of investment ideas used by financial professionals in the 1990s aren't applicable in today's markets.
- There is money you hope you'll have in the future, and there's money you know you'll have in the future. Make sure you know how much you need when you retire.
- Organizing your assets starts with making a list. You can then understand how each asset is balanced for risk.
- Your exposure to risk is ultimately determined by you.
- Use the Rule of 100 as a general guiding principle when determining how much risk your retirement investments should be exposed to (100 - [your age] = [percentage of your investments that can comfortably be exposed to risk]).

2

ARE YOU SWINGING
FOR THE FENCES?

Babe Ruth was a baseball phenom known for his ability to knock it out of the park. Most people don't realize that he missed the ball more times than he hit it. With a once-unbeatable record number of 714 homeruns during his career, he also held another record: more strikeouts than any other career hitter with a grand total of 1,330 strikeouts.*

These numbers remind us of what we often forget: when you step up to the plate intent on swinging for the fences, you're actually more likely to score a big zero. This wasn't a surprise to Babe Ruth himself, who when asked how to hit a homerun replied, "I hit big or I miss big." This philosophy of hitting big or missing

---

* *http://www.baseball-almanac.com/hitting/histrk1.shtml*

big is very similar to the approach investors take during their accumulation years when playing the stock market.

While taking big chances might be appropriate for someone making their name in the world or accumulating as many assets as possible in their 401(k), this philosophy doesn't bode well for someone approaching retirement. During retirement, you want to score consistently by hitting a regular number of singles and doubles to bring home the income, because during retirement, one strikeout could very well mean *game over.*

LINE UP YOUR DEFENSE

Over the course of your lifetime, it is likely that you have acquired a variety of assets. Assets can range from money that you have in a savings account or a 401(k), to a pension or an IRA. You have earned money and have made financial decisions based on the best information you had at the time. When viewed as a whole, however, you might not have an overall strategy for the management of your assets. As we have seen, it's more important than ever to know which of your assets are at risk. High market volatility and low treasury rates make for challenging financial topography. Navigating this financial landscape starts with planful asset management that takes into account your specific needs and options.

Even if you feel that you have plenty of money in your 401(k) or IRA, not knowing how much *risk* those investments are exposed to can cause you major financial suffering. Take the market crash of 2008 for example. In 2008, the average investor lost 30 percent of their 401(k). If more people had shifted their investments away from risk as they neared retirement age using the Rule of 100, they may have lost a lot less money going into retirement.

Nobody worries much about their investments when the stock market is performing well, because generally speaking, when the market is good, everybody makes money. We like to find out how a fund or stock does when the market is bad. How would your current portfolio hold up if, for example, another downturn came along like the one we saw in 2001 or 2002, or another recession like the one we saw in '08 and early '09? How would you feel about losing money as a retiree? What would happen to your income if your portfolio went down by 50 percent?

Those are the kinds of questions you need to answer when preparing for the long stretch of time that could be your retirement game. Athletes often do drills and run plays on the practice field to help them prepare for the game. As an investor, you can do the same kind of thing to test your portfolio and risk tolerance before a win or loss actually occurs. These exercises are designed to take the complicated working parts of investments and make them simple.

THE RISK EXERCISE

The first exercise is a risk test designed to measure your ability to stomach a hit, so you can determine whether or not you want to keep these investments in play.

Using a sheet of paper, draw three different squares and label them as your "buckets".

- **Bucket #1 is safe and secure.** The dollars you put into this bucket are guaranteed not to lose any principal, and you can know with some degree of certainty that the money will be there when you need it. Investments in this bucket might include bank CDs and savings accounts, fixed annuities, fixed indexed annuities, money market accounts, and US Savings Bonds.
- **Bucket #2 is low-moderate risk.** You would hope that most of the money allocated to this bucket would be there in a five to ten year time frame when you need to draw on the funds, but there is a low to moderate risk that

you could lose money. Investments in this bucket might include bonds or a managed account.

- **Bucket #3 is high risk.** You plan to hold investments in this bucket for a five to ten year time frame or longer in the hopes of earning a higher return, but there is also an increased risk of losing money. Investments in this bucket might include mutual funds, stocks and REITs.

Now, using your collection of investing dollars, if you had your choice, what percentage of your money would you put where? For example, if the sum total of your retirement savings were $400,000, what percent of that money would you put into bucket number one? What percent in bucket number two? How about bucket number three?

There is no right or wrong answer to this question, and answers are often all over the board. In situations involving couples, it's often the case that the husband and wife will have their money allocated very differently from each other. The real surprise comes later, however, when we compare the bucket exercise with the reality of how your money is actually positioned.

THE STRESS TEST

This next exercise is designed to test your portfolio. After a financial professional has gathered all the data about your different holdings, he or she can use sophisticated computer software to analyze your portfolio's performance. There are many different kinds of tests that a professional can run for you to determine fund performance and fee structure. The Stress Test takes a look at the entire portfolio and projects certain scenarios such as a slowdown in the economy in China, or an interest rate increase by the Federal Reserve or a market correction similar to what we saw in 2008. The software generates these different scenarios and tests how your current portfolio would perform under these various stresses. How would your investments hold up? What would change? How would those changes affect you and your ability to maintain a steady income? Better to look at all of this now, on paper, before it becomes the reality in your retirement account.

One key indicator in particular that you want to pay attention to is the maximum drawdown. The maximum drawdown is a way to measure market loss using the period of time from when the market peaks, to its lowest point. Said another way, it is simply a top-to-bottom loss. For example, during the Great Recession of 2008, your broker may have told you that your loss was 20 or 30 percent, but what was the period of time used to calculate that loss? Using the maximum drawdown, we see that the average investor lost 59 percent from the high point in 2007 to the low point in 2009.* If you consider a fifty percent loss on top of the 4 to 5 percent you want to draw out annually for income, then you can see how this would be a recipe for running out of money before you run out of life.

THE COLOR OF MONEY EXERCISE

Going a step further, we can use color to organize the types of investments and assets you have in your portfolio to create a helpful visual schematic. While the Risk Exercise allowed you to choose the risk you were exposed to, and the Stress Test looked at projected risk, the Color of Money exercise here helps you visualize your current risk.

For our purposes here, we have two kinds of money:
- Know So Money (which is safer and more dependable) is green.
- Hope So Money (which is exposed to risk and fluctuates with the market) is red.

---

* *Peace of Mind Planning, Roccy DeFrancesco, JD, CWPP, CAPP, CMP, 2014*

A financial professional can help you better understand the color of the money in your investment portfolio.

The fact of the matter is that a lot of people don't know their level of exposure to risk. Visually organizing your assets is an important and powerful way to get a clear picture of what kind of money you have, where it is, and how you can best use it in the future. This process is as simple as listing your assets and assigning them a color based on their status as Know So or Hope So Money. Work with your financial professional to create a comprehensive inventory of your assets to understand what you are working with before making any decisions. This may be the first time you have ever sat down and sorted out all of your assets, allowing you to see how much money you have at risk in the market. Comparing the color of your investments will give you an idea of how near or far you are from adhering to the Rule of 100.

When using the Rule of 100 to calculate your level of risk, your financial age might be different than your chronological age. The way you organize your assets depends on your goals and your level of comfort with risk. Whatever you determine the appropriate amount of risk for you to be, you will need to organize your portfolio to reflect your goals. If you have more Red Money than Green Money, in particular, you will need to make decisions

Green Money	Red Money
"Green Money" is safer.	**"Red Money" is at risk.**
This is money that offers a minimum guarantee but it may pose risks other than market risk.	**This is money that can go up or down in value. It may pose risk if it is not properly managed to serve a specific purpose in a comprehensive plan.**

about how to move it. You can work with a financial professional to find appropriate Green Money options for your situation.

OPTIMIZING RISK AND FINDING THE RIGHT BALANCE

The next step is to know the right amount and ratio of Green and Red Money for you at your stage of retirement planning.

Investing heavily in Red Money and gambling all of your assets on the market is incredibly risky no matter where you fall within the Rule of 100. Money in the market can't be depended on to generate income, and a plan that leans too heavily on Red Money can easily fail, especially when investment decisions are influenced by emotional reactions to market downturns and recoveries. Not only is this an unwise plan, it can be incredibly stressful to an investor who is gambling everything on stocks and mutual funds.

But a plan that uses too much Green Money avoids all volatility and can also fail. Why? Investing all of your money in Certificates of Deposit (CDs), savings accounts, money markets and other low return accounts may provide interest and income, but that likely won't be enough to keep pace with inflation. If you focus exclusively on income from Green Money and avoid owning any stocks or mutual funds in your portfolio, you won't be able to leverage the potential for long-term growth your portfolio needs to stay healthy and productive. This is where the Rule of 100 can help you determine how much of your money should be invested in the market to anticipate your future needs.

Green Money becomes much more important as you age. While you want to reduce the amount of Red Money you have and to transition it to Green Money, you don't necessarily need all of it to generate income for you right away. Taking a closer look at your money, you will see that you can divide your money up according to when you will need it and what you will need it for:

» *Ron and Amanda retire with a total of $400,000 in assets including their 401(k) portfolio and their money in the bank. After organizing their assets according to the Color of Money, the couple realizes they have much more Red Money than they are comfortable with. They recognize the need to move some of their Red Money over to Green Money, but how much?*

When they did the Risk Test together, Amanda placed 95 percent of their money in the safe and secure Bucket number one; Ron, on the other hand, enjoys playing the stock market and sees the need for some accumulation. He put 50 percent of their money in bucket number one and the other 50 percent spread out over buckets two and three.

As a first step in reallocating their assets, their financial professional asks them, "Out of that $400,000, how much money do you want to keep in the bank or credit union where it's liquid and easy to get to?"

Ron and Amanda look at each other. Both of them remember how the water heater went out last month, flooded their basement, and caused over $10,000 worth of damage to the floors and walls, not to mention the cost of replacing the water heater itself.

"This is your rainy day fund," the professional explains. "You want this to be Green Money because you'll need to know the money will be there when you need it. What will make you feel comfortable? The range is anywhere from $5,000 to $100,000."

Ron and Amanda decide they want to put $25,000 in their rainy day fund. Now that this money has a specific purpose, that leaves them with $375,000 to work with. Upon closer examination, however, they discover that this amount can also be broken down depending on when they will need the money.

TYPES OF GREEN MONEY:
NEED NOW AND NEED LATER

Money that you need to depend on for income and emergency spending is Green Money. Most investors like Ron and Amanda discover that *there are two types of Green Money:* money used for income now and money used for accumulation to meet your income needs in five, 10 or 20 years.

- **Money needed for income is Need Now Money.** It is money you need to meet your basic needs, to pay your bills, your mortgage if you have one and the costs associated with maintaining your lifestyle.

- **Money used for accumulation is Need Later Money.** It's money that you don't need now for income, but will need to rely on down the road. Depending on your stomach for risk, you might still want to think of this as Green Money because you will rely on it later for income and will need to count on it being there. There is another type of money (Yellow Money) that can be used to generate Need Later funds. Yellow Money is Red Money under the watchful eye of a professional and is the subject of Chapter 7. Need Later Money represents income your assets will need to generate for future use. When planning your retirement, it is vital to decide how much of your assets to structure for income and how much to set aside to accumulate to create Need Later Money.

You must figure out if your income and accumulation needs are met. Your Need Now and Need Later Money are top priorities. Need Now Money, in particular, will dictate what your options for future needs are.

DRAWING UP THE PLAYS

Determining the amount of risk that is right for you depends on your specific situation. It starts by examining your particular financial position.

The Rule of 100 is a useful way to begin to deliberate the right amount of risk for you. But remember, it's just a baseline. Use it as a starting point for figuring out where your money should be. If you're a 60-year-old investor, the Rule of 100 suggests that you have 60 percent Green Money and 40 percent Red Money. There are many reasons why someone might be more risk tolerant, not the least of which is feeling young! Experienced investors, people who feel they need to gamble for a higher return, or people who have met their retirement income goals and are looking for additional ways to accumulate wealth are all candidates for investment strategies that incorporate higher levels of risk. In the end, it comes down to your personal tolerance and appetite for risk. How much are you willing to lose?

Consulting with a financial professional is often the wisest approach to calculating your risk level. A professional can help determine your risk tolerance by getting to know you, asking you a set of questions and even giving you a survey or a test to determine your comfort level with different types of risk. Here's a typical scenario a financial professional might pose to you:

"You have $100,000 saved that you would like to invest in the market. There is an investment product that could turn your $100,000 into $120,000. That same option, however, has the potential of losing you up to $30,000, leaving you with $70,000."

Is that a scenario that you are willing to enter into? Or are you more comfortable with this one:

"You could turn your $100,000 into $110,000, but have the potential of losing $15,000, leaving you with $85,000."

Your answer to these and others types of questions will help a financial professional determine what level of risk is right for you.

They can then offer you investment strategies and management plans that reflect your financial age.

THE NUMBERS DON'T LIE

When the rubber meets the road, the numbers dictate your options. Your risk tolerance is an important indicator of what kinds of investments you should consider, but if the returns from those investments don't meet your retirement goals, your income needs will likely not be met. For example, if the level of risk you are comfortable with manages your investments at a 4 percent return and you need to realize an 8 percent return, your income needs aren't going to be met when you need to rely on your investments for retirement income. A professional may encourage you to be more aggressive with your investment strategy by taking on more risk in order to give you the potential of earning a greater return. If taking more risk isn't an option that you are comfortable with, then the discussion will turn to how you can earn more money or spend less in order to align your needs with your resources more closely.

How are you going to structure your income flow during retirement? The answer to this question dictates how you determine your risk tolerance. If the numbers say that you need to be more aggressive with your investing, or that you need to modify your lifestyle, it becomes a choice you need to make.

WORKING WITH AN INCOME SPECIALIST

Take a moment to think about your income goals:

What is your lifestyle today? Would you like to maintain it into retirement? Are you meeting your needs? Are you happy with your lifestyle? What do you really *need* to live on when you retire?

Some people will have the luxury of maintaining or improving their lifestyle, while others may have to make decisions about what they need versus what they want during their retirement.

Organizing your assets, understanding the color of your money, and creating an income and accumulation plan for retirement can quickly become an overwhelming task. The fact of the matter is that financial professionals build their careers around understanding the different variables affecting retirement financing.

Working with a Registered Investment Advisor held to the fiduciary standard means working with a professional who is legally obligated to help you make financial decisions that are in your best interest and fall within your comfort zone. Much like coaches who make decisions based on the best interest of the team, fiduciaries provide advice based on what's in the best interest of their clients. In fact, they have a legal obligation to do so. Investment advice from a fiduciary professional trained to help you maximize your retirement income will likely be different than the advice you get from professionals such as brokers who are trained to help you grow your money. Part of this difference has to do with the legal standards your professional is held to.

Suitability standards dictate that an advisor can recommend any financial product as long as it could be considered suitable to your individual situation. As you can imagine, the word suitable invites a lot of gray area, and what's helpful during your working years may actually be harmful during your distribution years.

Fiduciary standards require that an advisor always act in the best interest of his or her client at all times. Investment Advisor Representatives are also independent. The high standards they are held to require they have the ability to access whatever options are in their client's best interest. An investment advisor strives to:

- Put your interests first.
- Understand your specific financial situation.
- Offer straightforward advice that reflects your long-term goals.
- Recommend investment solutions that best fit your unique needs.

To this end, investment advisors are able to put together comprehensive retirement plans using more than one kind of investment.

Earlier we talked about how much more difficult it is to get anywhere when you keep your head down, eyes focused on every little step. Sometimes as a retiree, all the details of different investments can get overwhelming. As the person responsible for the success of your retirement, it is right to do your due diligence, to ask questions and make sure that you understand your investments and their purpose before choosing them for your portfolio. That being said, when you work with a fiduciary, you can have a greater degree of trust that your professional is putting together a plan that is in your best interest. You don't have to get lost in the rules and regulations, because that's the job of your professional. As long as you understand the play and are comfortable with it, you can retire with a greater degree of confidence, knowing that someone qualified has your back.

CHAPTER 2 RECAP //

- Multiple investment accounts can create confusion about risk and reward. Taking control of your assets begins with determining your exposure to risk. With the help of a financial professional, you can perform a Risk Exercise to test your risk appetite or run a Stress Test to test the ability of your portfolio to perform during economic turmoil.

- Assigning colors to money can help you more easily visualize the assets that make up your retirement savings. Green Money is safer and more reliable, Red Money represents assets that are exposed to risk, and Yellow Money is Red Money managed by a professional.

- Registered Investment Advisors held to the fiduciary standards of liability are legally obligated to always act in the best interest of their client. A fiduciary who specializes in retirement income planning can help you make decisions about your Red and Green Money that best reflect the goals of someone currently in or entering into their distribution years.

3

CREATING AN INCOME PLAN

The moment your working income ceases and you start living off the money you've set aside for retirement is what I call the "retirement cliff". When you begin drawing income from your retirement assets, you have entered the distribution phase of your financial plan. *The distribution phase of your retirement plan* is when you reach the point of relying on your assets for income. This is where your Green Money comes into play: the safer, more reliable assets that you have accumulated that are designed to provide you with a steady income. On day one of your retirement, you will need a steady and reliable supply of income from your Green Money

Every financial strategy for retirement needs first to accommodate the day-to-day need for income.

Satisfying that need for daily income entails first knowing how much you need, how much you have and who this money must provide for.

KEEP YOUR EYE ON THE BALL

Most people don't have a realistic idea about what they are spending each month to keep their household running. When planning for the 20 to 30 years that make up a retirement, we want to take a close look at ALL the expenses. Keeping your eye on the income ball, so to speak, will help you determine how to better allocate your assets for risk.

It's common for investors nearing retirement to think that once they stop working, their income needs will go down. What financial professionals in the industry often find, however, is that this isn't the case, especially when you factor in the increase of dining out, travelling (near or far) and the cost of health care. It's true that some expenses do go down during retirement, but other expenses go up, and it will be different for every situation.

Aside from the regular everyday expense of groceries, utilities, the mortgage if you have one, insurance and taxes, you also want to budget for the nicer things in life such as travel, vacations, birthday gifts and Christmas presents. Even if you own your home, you also have to budget for property taxes, which, in the state of Ohio, have to be paid twice a year. There might also be credit card debt and car payments to factor in.

Your financial professional can walk you through this process if you need assistance. After determining your annual income need, it is wise to aim for a slightly higher number. Say, for instance, you calculate your target income at $5,000 a month; a financial professional will look at that number and suggest an income around $6,000 so you can continue to replenish that rainy-day fund we talked about earlier. As a working person, you had your monthly expenses, but you typically earned more than their sum total. Most people want to keep the lifestyle they are accustomed to once they retire.

DIG DEEP

The moment you stop working and start living off the money that you've set aside for retirement is the day your distribution years begin. How are you going to replace the income that was once supplied by your paycheck? You may have a pension, an IRA or Roth IRA, dividends from stock holdings, money from the sale of real estate, rental property, or other sources of income. What other sources of reliable income do you have?

Most Americans can rely on their Social Security benefit as one Green Money source of income. In 2014, over 59 million Americans received almost $863 billion in Social Security benefits, with an average benefit of $1,294 a month.* This accounts for 38 percent of an average retiree's income.** This means that most people have to supply the remaining 62 percent of their income needs on their own, using a pension (if they are lucky enough to have one) and the investments they have saved.

If your monthly Social Security check and your other guaranteed income leaves a shortfall in your *desired* income, how are you going to fix it?

This shortfall is called the **Income Gap** and it needs to be filled in order to maintain your lifestyle into retirement. You also want to know how to fill that income gap with the fewest dollars possible. You basically want to buy that income gap for the least amount of money possible. You don't want it to cost you too much, because you want to get the most out of your other assets, including planning for your future and planning for your legacy. You do that by maximizing your Social Security benefit, leverag-

---

* *http://www.ssa.gov/news/press/basicfact.html*
** *http://www.ssa.gov/news/press/basicfact.html*

ing your additional income and looking at other investment tools that can help generate income for you. A professional, of course, should analyze your specific needs.

TAKING CARE OF YOUR TEAMMATE

Most people work hard so they can take care of the people they love. For married couples, you might say that it was a team effort getting here to this point in your life. Both of you contributed to your retirement savings in one way or another, and now you are both retiring. Even if one spouse doesn't want to be involved in the planning process, the responsible thing to do is to look at what the income picture would look like were one spouse to pass away. This is the part of planning known as *spousal continuation.*

In the case of married couples, statistics tell us that the person most likely to die first is the husband. While no one likes to talk about losing their spouse, looking at these statistics will likely motivate you to muscle through a plan. Women tend to outlive men by a good five years and in many cases, the woman is also younger than the man she marries.* Of the 800,000 people who lose their spouse annually, 700,000 of them are women, and according the U.S. Census Bureau, women can expect to be living alone for an average of 14 years.** The Social Security Administration also reports that poverty among women after the loss of a spouse continues to rise because so many people fail to prepare.***

As part of your comprehensive plan, your financial professional will take a look at how your cash flow situation would change when one spouse passes away. Is there a loss of a pension or a Social Security benefit check? What bills will change and what will stay the same? It's not uncommon to see a 30 to 60 percent

---

* *http://www.foxnews.com/health/2014/10/23/5-reasons-women-live-longer-than-men/*
** *http://www.widowshope.org/first-steps/these-are-the-statistics/*
*** *http://www.ssa.gov/policy/docs/ssb/v65n3/v65n3p31.html*

reduction in income after one spouse passes away, without a corresponding reduction of expenses.

There is a misperception out there that when one spouse passes away, your expenses will go down.

What happens instead is that your income changes significantly but your lifestyle does not. You still have the same car insurance, the same cable bill and utilities. Your taxes will either stay the same or go up as you move from a married-filing-joint status to a single-filing status. Maybe your grocery bill is lower, but many widows find they need to socialize more and go out for their meals. It's not uncommon for expenses to even increase. A good income plan takes all of this into account and puts together a plan to fix this problem so your teammate is covered.

The first place we look to improve your chances of maintaining your lifestyle is Social Security. Spousal benefits as offered through Social Security give you the option of choosing the larger of the two benefit checks should your spouse pass away. For married couples, maximizing the larger of the two amounts during the planning phase is one way to increase chances that the surviving spouse will be able to make ends meet. This means working with a financial professional to determine which filing strategy will pay out the highest lifetime amount. Most people don't even realize these filing strategies exist. A Social Security Maximization Report—talked about in the next chapter—can show you how to maximize this important lifetime benefit.

So, how do you figure out how much you need, how much you have and how that money can provide for both you and your spouse? When you take health care costs, potential emergencies, plans for moving or traveling, and other retirement expenses into account, you can really give your calculator a workout. You want to maximize retirement benefits to meet your lifetime income needs. An Investment Advisor can help you answer those questions by working with you to customize an income plan.

CHAPTER 3 RECAP //

- Every retirement plan must address the day-to-day need for paying the bills. The foundation of an income plan depends on knowing how much money you need and when you need it.
- Spousal continuation is one area often overlooked by retirees. When one spouse dies, the loss of pensions and monetary benefits such as Social Security means a reduction in monthly income. Working with a qualified professional can help you make decisions now to make this transition easier from a financial standpoint.

4

UNDERSTANDING SOCIAL SECURITY

One kind of Green Money that most Americans rely on for income when they retire is Social Security. If you're like most Americans, Social Security is or will be an important part of your retirement income and one that you should know how to properly manage. As a first step in creating your income plan, a financial professional will take a look at your Social Security benefit options. Social Security is the foundation of income planning for anyone who is about to retire and is a reliable source of Green Money in your overall income plan.

> » *Elizabeth had worked full-time nearly her entire adult life and was looking forward to enjoying retirement with her husband, kids and grandkids. When she turned 62, she decided*

to take advantage of her Social Security benefits as soon as they became available.

A couple of years later, she was organizing some of the paperwork in her home office. She came across an old Social Security statement, and remembered the feeling of filing and beginning a new phase in her life.

However, as she looked over the statement, she realized in retrospect that she might have been better off waiting to file for benefits. She had saved enough to wait for benefits, and if she had, her monthly benefit could have been quite a bit more.

When she was in the process of retiring, there were so many other decisions to make. It seemed very straightforward to file right away. She made a note to call the Social Security Administration to see if it was possible to change her monthly benefit to the larger amount.

Here are some facts that illustrate how Americans currently use Social Security:

- Nearly 90 percent of Americans age 65 and older receive Social Security benefits.*
- Social Security provides about 39 percent of the income of the elderly.*
- Claiming Social Security benefits at the wrong time can reduce your monthly benefit by up to 65 percent.**
- In 2013, 36 percent of men and 40 percent of women claimed Social Security benefits at age 62.***

---

* *http://www.ssa.gov/pressoffice/basicfact.htm*

** *https://www.ssa.gov/planners/retire/retirechart.html*

*** *Trends in Social Security Claiming, Alicia H Munnell and Anqi Chen, Center for Retirement Research, May 2015. http://crr.bc.edu/wp-content/uploads/2015/05/IB_15-8.pdf*

- In 2013, more than a third of workers claimed Social Security benefits as soon they became eligible.*
- In 2015, the average monthly Social Security benefit was $1,328. *The maximum benefit for 2015 was $2,663. The $1,335 monthly benefit reduction between the average and the maximum is applied for life.* **

There are many aspects of Social Security that are well known and others that aren't. When it comes time for you to cash in on your Social Security benefit, you will have many options and choices. Social Security is a massive government program that manages retirement benefits for millions of people. Experts spend their entire careers understanding and analyzing it. Luckily, you don't have to understand all of the intricacies of Social Security to maximize its advantages. You simply need to know the best way to manage your Social Security benefit. You need to know exactly what to do to get the most from your Social Security benefit and when to do it. Taking the time to create a roadmap for your Social Security strategy will help ensure that you are able to exact your maximum benefit and efficiently coordinate it with the rest of your retirement plan.

There are many aspects of Social Security that you have no control over. You don't control how much you put into it, and you don't control what it's invested in or how the government manages it. However, you do control when and how you file for benefits. The real question about Social Security that you need to answer is, "When should I start taking Social Security?" While

---

* *Trends in Social Security Claiming, Alicia H Munnell and Anqi Chen, Center for Retirement Research, May 2015. http://crr.bc.edu/wp-content/uploads/2015/05/IB_15-8.pdf*

** *https://www.ssa.gov/news/press/factsheets/colafacts2015.html*

this is the all-important question, there are a couple of key pieces of information you need to track down first.

Before we get into a few calculations and strategies that can make all the difference, let's start by covering the basic information about Social Security which should give you an idea of where you stand. Just as the foundation of a house creates the stable platform for the rest of the framework to rest upon, your Social Security benefit is an important part of your overall retirement plan. The purpose of the information that follows is not to give an exhaustive explanation of how Social Security works, but to give you some tools and questions to start understanding how Social Security affects your retirement and how you can prepare for it.

Let's start with eligibility.

Eligibility. Understanding how and when you are eligible for Social Security benefits will help clarify what to expect when the time comes to claim them.

To receive retirement benefits from Social Security, you must earn eligibility. In almost all cases, Americans born after 1929 must earn 40 quarters of credit to be eligible to draw their Social Security retirement benefit. In 2015, a Social Security credit represents $1,220 earned in a calendar quarter. The number changes as it is indexed each year, but not drastically. In 2014, a credit represented $1,200. Four quarters of credit is the maximum number that can be earned each year. In 2015, an American would have had to earn at least $4,880 to accumulate four credits. In order to qualify for retirement benefits, you must have earned a minimum number of credits. Additionally, if you are at least 62 years old and have been married to a recipient of Social Security benefits for at least 12 months, you can choose to receive Spousal Benefits. Although 40 is the minimum number of credits required to begin drawing benefits, it is important to know that once you claim your Social Security benefit, there is no going back. Although there may be cost of living adjustments made, you are locked into that base benefit amount forever.

Primary Insurance Amount. You can think of your Primary Insurance Amount (PIA) like a ripening fruit. It represents the amount of your Social Security benefit at your Full Retirement Age (FRA). Your benefit becomes fully ripe at your FRA, and will neither reduce nor increase due to early or delayed retirement options. If you opt to take benefits before your FRA, however, your monthly benefit will be less than your PIA. You will essentially be picking an unripe fruit. On the one hand, waiting until after your FRA to access your benefits will increase your benefit beyond your PIA. On the other hand, you don't want the fruit to overripen, because every month you wait is one less check you get from the government.

Full Retirement Age. Your FRA is an important figure for anyone who is planning to rely on Social Security benefits in their retirement. Depending on when you were born, there is a specific age at which you will attain FRA. Your FRA is dictated by your year of birth and is the age at which you can begin receiving your full monthly benefit. Your FRA is important because it is half of the equation used to calculate your Social Security benefit. The other half of the equation is based on when you start taking benefits.

When Social Security was initially set up, the FRA was age 65, and it still is for people born before 1938. But as time has passed, the age for receiving full retirement benefits has increased. If you were born between 1938 and 1960, your full retirement age is somewhere on a sliding scale between 65 and 67. Anyone born in 1960 or later will now have to wait until age 67 for full benefits. Increasing the FRA has helped the government reduce the cost of the Social Security program, which paid out almost $870 billion to beneficiaries in 2015!*

While you can begin collecting benefits as early as age 62, the amount you receive as a monthly benefit will be less than it would be if you wait until you reach or surpass your FRA. It is important to note that if you file for your Social Security benefit before your FRA, *the reduction to your monthly benefit will remain in place for the rest of your life.* You can also delay receiving benefits up to age 70, in which case your benefits will be higher than your PIA for the rest of your life.

- At FRA, 100 percent of PIA is available as a monthly benefit.
- At age 62, your Social Security retirement benefits are available. For each month you take benefits prior to your FRA, however, the monthly amount of your benefit is reduced. *This reduction stays in place for the rest of your life.*
- At age 70, your monthly benefit reaches its maximum. After you turn age 70, your monthly benefit will no longer increase.

Year of Birth	Full Retirement Age
1943-1954	66
1955	66 and 2 months
1956	66 and 4 months
1957	66 and 6 months
1958	66 and 8 months
1959	66 and 10 months
1960 or later	age 67**

---

* *https://www.ssa.gov/news/press/basicfact.html*
** *http://www.ssa.gov/OACT/progdata/nra.html*

ROLLING UP YOUR SOCIAL SECURITY

Your Social Security income "rolls up" the longer you wait to claim it. Your monthly benefit will continue to increase until you turn 70 years old. Even though Social Security is the foundation of most people's retirement, many Americans feel that they don't have control over how or when they receive their benefits. The truth is that every dollar you increase your Social Security income by means less money you will have to spend from your nest egg to meet your retirement income needs, but many retirees do not take advantage of this fact. For many people, creating their Social Security strategy is the most important decision they can make to positively impact their retirement. *The difference between the best and worst Social Security decision can be tens of thousands of dollars over a lifetime of benefits.*

Deciding NOW or LATER: Following the above logic, it makes sense to wait as long as you can to begin receiving your Social Security benefit. However, the answer isn't always that simple. Not everyone has the option of waiting. Many people need to rely on Social Security on day one of their retirement. Some might need the income. Others might be in poor health and don't feel they will live long enough to make waiting until their FRA worthwhile for themselves or their families. It is also possible, however, that the majority of folks taking an early benefit at age 62 are simply under-informed about Social Security. Perhaps they make this major decision based on rumors and emotion.

File Immediately if You:
- Find your job is unbearable.
- Are willing to sacrifice retirement income.
- Are not healthy and need a reliable source of income.

Consider Delaying Your Benefit if You:
- Want to maximize your retirement income.

- Want to increase retirement benefits for your spouse.
- Are still working and like it.
- Are healthy and willing / able to wait to file.

So if you decide to wait, how long should you wait? Lots of people can put it off for a few years, but not everyone can wait until they are 70 years old. Your individual circumstances may be able to help you determine when you should begin taking Social Security. If you do the math, you will quickly see that between ages 62 and 70, there are 96 months in which you can file for your Social Security benefit. If you take into account those 96 months and the 96 months your spouse could also file for Social Security, and the number of different strategies for structuring your benefit, you can easily end up with more than 20,000 different scenarios. It's safe to say this isn't the kind of math that most people can easily handle. Each month would result in a different benefit amount. The longer you wait, the higher your monthly benefit amount becomes. Each month you wait, however, is one less month that you receive a Social Security check.

The goal is to maximize your lifetime benefits. That may not always mean waiting until you can get the largest monthly payment. Taking the bigger picture into account, you want to find out how to get the most money out of Social Security over the number of years that you draw from it. Don't underestimate the power of optimizing your benefit: the difference between the BEST and WORST Social Security election can easily be worth thousands of dollars in lifetime benefits. *The difference can be very substantial!*

If you know that every month you wait, your Social Security benefit goes up a little bit, and you also know that every month you wait, you receive one less benefit check, how do you determine where the sweet spot is that maximizes your benefits over your lifetime? Financial professionals have access to software that will calculate the best year and month for you to file for benefits based on your default life expectancy. You can further customize that information by estimating your life expectancy based on your health, habits and family history. If you can then create an income plan (we'll get into this later in the chapter) that helps you wait until the target date for you to file for Social Security, you can optimize your retirement income strategy to get the most out of your Social Security benefit. How can you calculate your life expectancy? Well, you don't know exactly how long you'll live, but you have a better idea than the government does. They rely on averages to make their calculations. *You have much more personal information about your health, lifestyle and family history than they do.* You can use that knowledge to game the system and beat all the other people who are making uninformed decisions by filing early for Social Security.

While you can and should educate yourself about how Social Security works, the reality is you don't need to know a lot of general information about Social Security in order to make choices about your retirement. What you do need to know is exactly *what to do to maximize your benefit.* Because knowing what you need to do has huge impacts on your retirement! For most Americans, Social Security is the foundation of income planning for retirement. Social Security benefits represent about 39 percent of the income of the elderly.* For many people, it can represent the largest portion of their retirement income. Not treating your Social Security benefit as an asset and investment tool can lead to sub-optimization of your largest source of retirement income.

Let's take a look at an example that shows the impact of working with a financial professional to optimize Social Security benefits:

---

* *http://www.socialsecurity.gov/pressoffice/basicfact.htm*

» George and Mary Maloney are a typical American couple who have worked their whole lives and saved when they could. George is 60 years old, and Mary is 56 years old. They sat down with a financial professional who logged onto the Social Security website to look up their PIAs. George's PIA is $1,900 and Mary's is $900.

If the Maloney's cash in at age 62 and begin taking retirement benefits from Social Security, they will receive an estimated $568,600 in lifetime benefits. That may seem like a lot, but if you divide that amount over 20 years, it averages out to around $28,400 per year. The Maloney's are accustomed to a more significant annual income than that. To make up the difference, they will have to rely on alternative retirement income options. They will basically have to depend on a bigger nest egg to provide them with the income they need.

If they wait until their FRA, they will increase their lifetime benefits to an estimated $609,000. This option allows them to achieve their Primary Insurance Amount, which will provide them a $34,200 annual income.

After learning the Maloney's needs and using software to calculate the most optimal time to begin drawing benefits, the Maloney's financial professional determined that the best option for them drastically increases their potential lifetime benefits to $649,000!

*By using strategies that their financial professional recommended, they increased their potential lifetime benefits by as much as **$80,000.** There's no telling how much you could miss out on from your Social Security if you don't take time to create a strategy that calculates your maximum benefit. For the Maloney's, the value of maximizing their benefits was the difference between night and day. While this may seem like a special case, it isn't uncommon to find benefit increases of this* *magnitude. You'll never know unless you take a look at your own options.*

Despite the importance of knowing when and how to take your Social Security benefit, many of today's retirees and pre-retirees may know little about the mechanics of Social Security and how they can maximize their benefit.

So, to whom should you turn for advice when making this complex decision? Before you pick up the phone and call Uncle Sam, you should know that the Social Security Administration (SSA) representatives are actually prohibited from giving you election advice! Plus, SSA representatives in general are trained to focus on monthly benefit amounts, not the lifetime income for a family.

MAXIMIZING YOUR LIFETIME BENEFIT

As discussed in Chapter 2, calculating how to maximize **lifetime benefits** is more important than waiting until age 70 for your maximum **monthly benefit amount.** It's about getting the most income during your lifetime. Professional benefit maximization software can target the year and month that it is most beneficial for you to file based on your life expectancy.

The three most common ages that people associate with retirement benefits are 62 (Earliest Eligible Age), 66 (Full Retirement Age), and 70 (age at which monthly maximum benefit is reached). In almost all circumstances, however, none of those three most common ages will give you the maximum lifetime benefit.

Remember, every month you wait to file, the amount of your benefit check goes up, but you also get one less check. You don't know how exactly how long you're going to live, but you have a better idea of your life expectancy than the actuaries at the Social Security Administration who can only work with averages. They can't make calculations based on your specific situation. A professional can run the numbers for you and get the target date that maximizes your potential lifetime benefits. You can't get this information from the SSA, but you *can* get it from a financial professional.

Types of Social Security Benefits:
- *Retired Worker Benefit.* This is the benefit with which most people are familiar. The Retired Worker Benefit is what most people are talking about when they refer to Social Security. It is your benefit based on your earnings and the amount that you have paid into the system over the span of your career.
- *Spousal Benefit.* This is available to the spouse of someone who is eligible for Retired Worker Benefits.
- *Survivorship Benefit.* When one spouse passes away, the survivor is able to receive the larger of the two benefit amounts.
- *Restricted Application.* A higher-earning spouse may be able to start collecting a spousal benefit on the lower-earning spouse's benefit while allowing his or her benefit to continue to grow. Due to the Bipartisan Budget Act of 2015, this option is only available to individuals who turned age 62 before January 1, 2016.

In November of 2015, the Bipartisan Budget Act of 2015 was passed, which will have a dramatic impact on the way many Americans plan for Social Security. As the largest change to Social Security since 2000, the Bipartisan Budget Act of 2015 eliminated an estimated $9.5 billion* of benefits to retirees and may

---

* *http://www.nasdaq.com/article/congress-planning-to-close-social-security-loopholes-cm536252*

limit some of the flexibility you previously had to structure your benefits.

In 2000, Congress passed the Senior Citizens Freedom to Work Act. The bill allowed retirees to suspend receiving benefits so they wouldn't be subject to additional taxation if they chose to return to work after they filed for Social Security. However, by doing so, the bill also unintentionally created several loopholes in claiming strategies: most notably, the Restricted Application for spousal benefits and "file and suspend" filing strategy. For most Americans, the Bipartisan Budget Act of 2015 closed these loopholes by eliminating "file and suspend" and the Restricted Application.

The new rules mandate that:

- If a primary worker is not currently receiving benefits, then their dependents (child, spouse) can no longer collect benefits based on the primary worker's earning record.
- If you file for benefits, then you are filing for *all* benefits to which you are entitled—not just the benefit type you choose.

It's important to remember that in spite of these immense changes, one thing stayed the same—filing for Social Security is one of the most important financial decisions you will make in your lifetime, and a financial professional can help ensure you make the right one.

THE DIVORCE FACTOR

How does a divorced spouse qualify for benefits? If you have gone through a divorce, it might affect the retirement benefit to which you are entitled.

In general, a person can receive benefits as a divorced spouse on a former spouse's Social Security record so long as the following conditions are met:

- the marriage lasted at least 10 years; and
- the person filing for divorce benefits is at least age 62, unmarried, and not entitled to a higher Social Security benefit on his or her own record.*

With all of the different options, strategies and benefits to choose from, you can see why filing for Social Security is more complicated than just mailing in the paperwork. Gathering the data and making yourself aware of all your different options isn't enough to know exactly what to do, however. On the one hand, you can knock yourself out trying to figure out which options are best for you and wondering if you made the best decision. On the other hand, you can work with a financial professional who uses customized software that takes all the variables of your specific situation into account and calculates your best option. You have tens of thousands of different options for filing for your Social Security benefit. If your spouse is a different age than you are, it nearly doubles the amount of options you have. This is far more complicated arithmetic than most people can do on their own. If you want a truly accurate understanding of when and how to file, you need someone who will ask you the right questions about your situation, someone who has access to specialized software that can crunch the numbers. The reality is that you need to work with a professional that can provide you with the sophisticated analysis of your situation that will help you make a truly informed decision.

Important Questions about Your Social Security Benefit:
- *How can I maximize my lifetime benefit?* By knowing when and how to file for Social Security. This usually means waiting until you have at least reached your Full Retire-

---

* *http://www.ssa.gov/retire2/yourdivspouse.htm*

ment Age. A professional has the experience and the tools to help determine when and how you can maximize your lifetime benefits.

- *Who will provide reliable advice for making these decisions?* Only a professional has the tools and experience to provide you reliable advice.

- *Will the Social Security Administration provide me with the advice?* The Social Security Administration cannot provide you with advice or strategies for claiming your benefit. They can give you information about your monthly benefit, but that's it. They also don't have the tools to tell you what your specific best option is. They can accurately answer how the system works, but they can't advise you on what decision to make as to how and when to file for benefits.

The Maximization Report that your financial professional will generate represents an invaluable resource for understanding how and when to file for your Social Security benefit. When you get your customized Social Security Maximization Report, you will not only know all the options available to you—but you will understand the financial implications of each choice. In addition to the analysis, you will also get a report that shows *exactly* at what age—including which month and year—you should trigger benefits and how you should apply. It also includes a variety of other time-specific recommendations, such as when to apply for Medicare or take Required Minimum Distributions from your qualified plans. A report means there is no need to wonder, or to try to figure out when to take action—the Social Security Maximization Report lays it all out for you in plain English.

CHAPTER 4 RECAP //

- To get the most out of your Social Security benefit, you need to file at the right time.
- An Investment Advisor can help you determine when you should file for Social Security to get your Maximum Lifetime Benefit.
- A financial professional held to fiduciary standards of liability can help you determine when you should file for Social Security to get your Maximum Lifetime Benefit.

5

CREATE YOUR OWN
PENSION PLAN

The game of Black Jack is a popular and easy card game to play, found in every American gambling casino.* If you are familiar with this game (also known as 21), imagine for a moment that you are going to play at one of these casinos only you discover there are actually two versions of the game being offered. Which table would you rather sit at?

Table one is traditional Black Jack using $25 chips. You place your chip down, and if you win the hand against the dealer, not only do you get to keep your chip: you get another chip. You just won $25. But if you lose the hand, the dealer takes your chip, and you get nothing.

---

* *http://www.bicyclecards.com/how-to-play/blackjack/*

At table number two, the rules are different. You place your $25 chip down, and if you win the hand, instead of getting a $25 chip, you get a $15 chip. Now before you protest, here's the interesting thing about table number two: if you lose the hand, the dealer doesn't take your chip. Instead, you get to keep all your chips and continue playing for the opportunity to earn more. You can never lose your chips, and you can stay at the table for as long as you'd like.

Table one might sound more exciting, and you might for a time get really hot and lucky and make a whole lot more money, but you're also likely to lose more money. With table two, you can earn those chips, but no matter how long you stay in the game, and no matter what happens, you can't lose. This analogy aptly portrays the advantages being offered by today's hybrid annuities. This chapter will explain what they are, what they can do and why you might want to choose a different game when it comes to structuring yourself a guaranteed source of retirement income.

NOT YOUR FATHER'S ANNUITY

The phrase *hybrid annuity* is impossible to miss these days, especially if you are a retiree searching for a reliable way to secure income. What exactly is a hybrid annuity? Let's start with what it is NOT.

A hybrid annuity does NOT function like old annuities, such as one your father or grandfather might have had. These older-style annuities operated very much like a traditional pension in that they converted a lump sum of money into a stream of income guaranteed to pay for the rest of your life. If you lived until the age of 120, then you beat the insurance company. If you died the day after your payouts started, then all the money you paid into the annuity reverted back to the insurance company and they win. Hybrid annuities offer you a win-win situation: you can structure them for lifetime income, and when you pass away, any money left in the policy goes to your beneficiaries.

A hybrid annuity is NOT a variable annuity. It's important to make the distinction here because variable annuities often give all annuities a bad name. Variable annuities are a different creature altogether in that they are a Red Money annuity that can have unlimited growth invested in the stock market with a corresponding unlimited downside. Variable annuities also have high fees associated with them somewhere in the neighborhood of 2 to 4 percent. This type of annuity can be used to create an income, but it is really more useful as an accumulation tool that bets on an improving market. If you surrender a variable annuity, the insurance company will pay you the market value of the asset, regardless of whether it matches, exceeds or falls short of the value at which you bought the contract. If its value has dropped significantly, you may be better off taking the income payments without surrendering your contract.

It's NOT about whether the market goes up or down, but when it does. If it goes down at the wrong time for your five or 10-year retirement horizon, and you haven't guaranteed your income needs, then you could be in serious danger of losing your ability to maintain your lifestyle into retirement. Hybrid annuities give you a way to guarantee the income you need, which in effect gives you the ability to create your own pension.

Ask yourself the following questions:
- How concerned are you about finding a secure financial vehicle to protect your savings?
- How concerned are you that there may be a better way to structure your savings for income?

If you are concerned about the best way to fill your income gap, a fixed indexed annuity (aka hybrid annuity) is likely a good option for you. These hybrid annuities have many similar qualities to Social Security that give them the same look and feel as that reliable benefit check you get every month. If you could have the option to contribute more money toward Social Security in order to secure a guaranteed income, it would be a great way to create a Green Money asset that would enhance your retirement. Since that option isn't available, you may seek an investment tool that is similar to Social Security that provides you with a reliable income. It also has the potential to increase the value of your principal investment much like the winnings offered at the number two Black Jack table we talked about above.

TAKING A HYBRID APPROACH TO YOUR INCOME NEEDS

In the world of investor-speak, fixed indexed annuities (FIAs) go by many names. You'll see them referred to as a hybrid annuity, an income annuity or even an income annuity tool. We are just going to call them what they are: the FIA. The name explains it all.

- **Fixed**: The principle amount of your investment cannot go down in value due to market loss. It might go down in value due to your withdrawals, but that's not losing money, that's just distribution.
- **Indexed**: When you fund a contract with an insurance company in the form of an FIA, you are pegging your earnings on an index. It could be the S&P 500, the Dow Jones Industrial Average or any number of indexes. This index is what allows you to capture a portion of the market gains without participating in direct market loss.
- **Annuity**: An annuity investment can do what no other investment can do: structure you money in a way that provides you with a reliable income stream. One very unique feature of the FIA is that you are able to guarantee an income stream without having to annuitize the investment. Annuitization is when you trade in a lump

sum of money in return for a lifetime stream of income. Today's FIAs allow you to structure a lifetime stream of income using something called an Income Rider so you do not have to give up control of your money. An FIA without an income rider can still keep your principle safe and participate in market gains, making it a useful Green Money accumulation tool.

HOW THE FIA CAN FIT INTO YOUR INCOME PLAN

Here is how the FIA can create a pension that pays out benefits to you, your spouse and your beneficiaries:

When you put your money into an annuity, you are essentially buying an investment product from an insurance company. It is a contract between you and the insurance company that provides the investment tool.

Let's say you have saved $100,000 and need it to generate income to meet your needs above and beyond your Social Security and pension checks. You give the $100,000 to an insurance company, who in turn invests it to generate growth.

They usually select investments that have modest returns over long-term horizons. In other words, they generally put it somewhere stable and predictable. Most commonly, they will invest it in a combination of bonds and treasuries that are safer and dependable ways to grow money. They use the money from the insurance products they sell to invest, use a portion of the returns to generate profits for themselves, and return a portion to clients in the form of payouts, claims, and structured income options.

One of the most attractive qualities of these types of annuities is something called annual reset. Annual reset is sometimes also referred to as a "ratcheting." Instead of taking on the risk that comes with putting money in a fluctuating market, you can offset that risk onto the insurance company. It works like this: If the market goes down, you don't suffer a loss. Instead, the insurance company absorbs it. But if the market goes up, you share with the insurance company some of the profit made on the gain. The amount of gain you get is called your annuity participation rate. Typically the insurer will cap the amount of gain you can realize at somewhere between 3 and 7 percent. If the market goes up 10 percent, you would realize a portion of that gain (whatever percentage you are capped at). This means you never lose money on your investment, while always gaining a portion of the upswings. The measurement period of your annuity can be calculated monthly, weekly and even daily, but most annuities are measured annually. The level of the index when you buy and the index level one year later will determine the amount of gain. You and the insurance company are betting that the market will generally go up over time.

The following example shows just how helpful a fixed indexed annuity with an income rider can be for a retiree:

> » Bob and Susan are 62 years old and have decided to run the numbers to see what their retirement is going to look like. They know they currently need $6,000 per month to pay their bills and maintain their current lifestyle. They have also done their Social Security homework and have determined that, between the two of them, they will receive $4,200 per month in benefits. They also receive $350 per month in rent from a tenant who lives in a small carriage house in their backyard. Between their Social Security and the monthly rent income, they will be short $1,450 per month.
>
> They do have an additional asset, however. They have been contributing for years to an IRA that has reached a value of $350,000. They realize that they have to figure out how to turn the $350,000 in their IRA into $1,450 per month for the rest of their life. At first glance, it may seem like they will have plenty of money. With some quick calculations, they find

they have 240 months, or nearly 20 years, of monthly income before they exhaust the account. When you consider income tax, the potential for higher taxes in the future, and market fluctuations (because many IRAs are invested in the market), the amount in the IRA seems to have a little less clout. Every dollar Bob and Susan take out of the IRA is subject to income tax, and if they leave the remainder in the IRA, they run the risk of losing money in a volatile market. Once they retire and stop getting a paycheck every two weeks, they also stop contributing to their IRA. And when they aren't supplementing its growth with their own money, they are entirely dependent on market growth. That's a scary prospect. They could also withdraw the money from the IRA and put it in a savings account or CD, but removing all the money at once will put them in a tax bracket that will claim a huge portion of the value of the IRA. A seemingly straightforward asset has now become a complicated equation. Bob and Susan didn't know what to do, so they met with their financial professional.

Their financial professional suggested that they use the money to purchase an indexed annuity with an income rider. They selected an annuity that was designed for their specific situation. They took the lump sum from their IRA, placed it in an indexed annuity taking advantage of annual reset so they never lost the value of their investment. In return, they were guaranteed the $1,450 of income per month that they needed to meet their retirement goals. The simplicity of the contract allowed them to do an analysis with their professional just once to understand the product. They basically put their money in an investment crockpot where they didn't have to look at it or manage it. They just needed to let it simmer. In fact, their professional was able to find an annuity for them that allowed them their $1,450 monthly payment with a lump sum of $249,455, leaving them more than $100,000 *to reinvest somewhere else. Keep in mind that annuities are tax deferred, meaning you will pay tax on the income you receive from an annuity in the year you receive it.*

NOTHING BUT NET: HOW THE INCOME RIDER WORKS

To generate income from an FIA, you select something called an income rider. An income rider is a subset of an indexed annuity. To indulge yet again in our coaching metaphor, you might think of the income rider as one way to score even more points because it gives you essentially two kinds of nets: the swish of guaranteed returns with an accelerated growth rate and the safety net knowing that even if the market performs poorly, your income is calculated using the higher of the two accounts. Why the two accounts? In order to achieve this gains-with-protection, the purchase of an income rider creates a second account, and unless this is explained, it can (and does) create a lot of confusion.

The account value listed as your *income rider account* is a larger number than what your investment is actually worth, which is called *the account value*. When you elect to purchase the income rider, the fee you pay guarantees that your money will increase at a guaranteed rate, rolling up much like Social Security benefits over time. This account is what can provide you with a source for greater potential income.

To keep things simple, let's look at the two accounts created by the income rider:

The Income Rider Account is the value of the money growing in the separate account created by the income rider. This is NOT money you can access as a lump sum, but rather this is what you access on a monthly basis. This is also what the insurance company uses to calculate what your monthly payment will be (unless the actual account value is higher). The value of this account grows at a guaranteed higher rate and can never drop, but you are also unable to access this money except through regular income payments.

The Account Value reflects the actual value of your annuity account. This is money that you *can* access and this account can be emptied. If you elect to purchase an income rider and the actual account value drops to zero due to your distributions, the income rider gives you a safety net and you are still guaranteed your monthly income payment. Your principal is also guaranteed, so when the market goes up, you participate in a portion of the upside. When the market goes down, you don't participate in the downside and your account balance holds steady.

FIAs do offer some access to liquidity. In general, you can withdraw up to 10 percent of your money annually after the first 12 months without penalty or surrender charges. You are also free to walk away with your money once the contract is up, usually

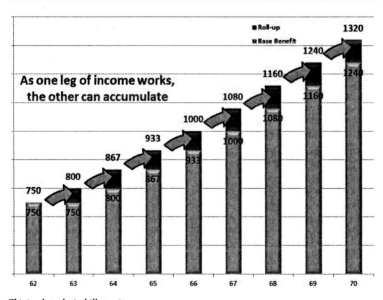

As one leg of income works, the other can accumulate

This is a hypothetical illustration

in seven to 10 years. If you purchase an income rider, you can guarantee both the ability to surrender the contract and to generate an income for a set period of years. As mentioned earlier, any money left in the annuity at the time of your death is passed on to your beneficiaries.

WHY THERE ARE SURRENDER CHARGES

As the insurance company holds your money and invests it, they generate a return on it that they use to pay you a regular monthly income based on a higher number. The insurance company has to outperform the amount that they pay you in order to make a profit.

Remember, insurance companies make long-term investments that provide them with predictable flows of money. They like to stabilize the amount of money that goes in and out of their doors instead of paying and receiving large unpredictable chunks at once. When you opt for an income rider, an insurance company can reliably predict how much money they will pay out to you over a set period of time. It's predictable, and they like that. They can base their business on those predictable numbers.

In order to encourage investors to leave their money in their annuity contracts, insurance companies create surrender periods that protect their investments. If you remove your money from the annuity contract during the surrender period, you will pay a penalty and will not be able to receive your entire investment amount back.

A typical surrender period is 10 years. If after three years you decide that you want your $100,000 back, the insurance company has that money tied up in bonds and other investments with the understanding that they will have it for another seven years. Because they will take a hit on removing the money from their investments prematurely, you will have to pay a surrender charge that makes up for their loss. During the surrender period, an annuity is not a demand deposit account like a savings or checking account. The higher returns that you are guaranteed from an annuity are dependent on the timeframe you selected. The longer an insurance company can hold your money, the easier it is for them to guarantee a predictable return on it.

If you leave your money in the annuity contract, you get a reliable monthly income no matter what happens in the market. Once the surrender period has expired, you can remove your money whenever you want. Your money becomes liquid again because the insurance company has used it in an investment that fit the timeline of your surrender period. For many people, this is an attractive trade off that can provide a creative solution for filling their income gap.

When is an annuity with an income rider right for you? A good financial professional can help you make that determination by taking the time to listen closely to your situation and understanding what your needs are as you enter retirement. Every advisor has a bag full of brochures and PowerPoint presentations, but they need to know exactly what the financial concerns of their individual clients are in order to help them make the most informed and beneficial decision. Some people need income today; others need it in five or 10 years. Others may have their income needs met but are planning to move closer to their children and will need to buy a house in 10 years. Or, if you want income in 15 years, you might want to choose a different investment product for 10 years, and then switch to an annuity with an income rider during the last five years of your timeline. Everyone's situation is different and everyone's needs are different. People who are interested in annuities, however, usually need to make decisions that affect their income needs, whether it is filling their income gap, or providing for income down the road.

What happens if you place on a shorter timeframe those assets from which you need to draw an income? Something called single premium immediate annuities may be for you:

SINGLE PREMIUM IMMEDIATE ANNUITIES (SPIA)

A single premium immediate annuity is simply a contract between you and an insurance company. SPIAs are structured so that you pay a lump sum of money (a single premium) to an insurance company, and they give you a guaranteed income over an agreed upon time period. That time period could be five years, or it could be for the remainder of your lifetime. Guarantees from insurance companies are based on the claims-paying ability of the issuing insurance company.

SPIAs provide investors with a stream of reliable income when they can't afford to take the risk of losing money in a fluctuating market. It should be noted, however, that in exchange for this reliable income, you do have to annuitize the money and give up lump-sum access to your funds. SPIAs operate more like the old-style annuities, so if you want to provide for a spouse in the event of your passing, you will want to ask your financial professional about your options for doing so. SPIAs do offer benefits and features that can provide for a joint-for-life income for married persons, and they offer tax advantages. Your financial professional can walk you through a series of different payment options to help you select the one that most closely fits your needs.

Additional Annuity Information:
- Some contracts will allow you to draw income from the high water mark that the market reaches each year. The income rider will then begin calculating its value from the high water mark.
- Variable annuities, however, can lose money with market fluctuations. As their name suggests, they vary with the

market. These annuities do not take advantage of annual reset when the market goes down. The income rider will stay the same, but the value of your actual contract may fall. If you surrender the annuity, the insurance company will pay you the market value of the asset, regardless of whether it matches, exceeds or falls short of the value at which you bought the contract. If its value has dropped significantly, you may be better off taking the income rider without surrendering your contract.

- Fixed index annuities are investment tools that look and feel a bit like Social Security. Every year you allow the money to grow with the market, and it will "roll up" by a specific amount, paying out a specific percent to you as income each year.

- Annuities can work very well to create income, and a financial professional can help you find the one that best matches your income need, and can also structure it to work perfectly for you.

The following story illustrates how using more than one kind of annuity can be helpful for a retiree.

> » Jean is 60 years old and is wondering how she can use her assets to provide her with a retirement income. She has a $5,000 per month income need. If she starts withdrawing her Social Security benefit in six years at age 66, it will provide her with $2,200 per month. She also has a pension that kicks in at age 70 that will give her another $1,320 per month.
>
> That leaves an income gap of $2,800 from ages 66 to 69, and then an income gap of $1,480 at age 70 and beyond. If Jean uses only Green Money to solve her income need, she will need to deposit $918,360 at 2 percent interest to meet her monthly goal for her lifetime. If she opts to use Red Money

and withdraws the amount she needs each month from the market, let's say the S & P 500, she will run out of cash in 10 years if she invested between the years of 2000 and 2012. Suffering a market downturn like that during the period for which she is relying on it for retirement income will change her life, and not for the better.

Working with a financial professional to find a better way, Jean found that she could take a hybrid approach to fill her income gap. Her professional recommended two different income vehicles: one that allowed her to deposit just $190,161 with a 2 percent return, and one that was a $146,000 fixed indexed annuity. These tools filled her income gap with $336,161, requiring her to spend $582,000 less money to accomplish her goal! Working with a professional to find the right tools for her retirement needs saved Jean over half a million dollars.

CREATING AN INCOME PLAN

Creating an income plan before you retire allows you to satisfy your need for lifetime income and ensures that your lifestyle can last as long as you do. You also want to create a plan that operates in the most efficient way possible. Doing so will give more security to your Need Later Money and will potentially allow you to build your legacy down the road.

Here is a basic roadmap of what we have covered so far:

- Review your income needs and look specifically at the shortfall you may have during each year of your retirement based on your Social Security income, and income from any other assets you have.
- Ask yourself where you are in your distribution phase. Is retirement one year away? 10 years away? Last year?
- Determine how much money you need and how you need to structure your existing assets to provide for that need.

- If you have an asset from which you need to generate income, consider options offered by purchasing an income rider on an annuity.

CHAPTER 5 RECAP //

- Today's Fixed Indexed Annuities (also called hybrid annuities, income annuities or the FIA) offer retirees a guaranteed income stream without annuitization. They function in a similar way to your Social Security benefit. With the FIA, any money left in the account once you die is sent to your named beneficiaries.
- The FIA is a Green Money asset that provides you with a guarantee of your principle. This means you cannot lose money due to a stock market downturn. This is not to be confused with the variable annuity, which is a Red Money asset whose principle can drop significantly due to stock market loss.
- Although the FIA is an income-producing asset that does not subject your income to market risk, it still has the opportunity to grow. FIAs participate in linked market growth without direct market loss through a strategy known as indexing. Indexing, combined with the power of annual reset, gives you both growth and safety of your principal.
- When you purchase an income rider with an FIA, you create a second account that grows at a higher rate. This guarantees your income, gives you access to your money, and gives money to your beneficiaries.
- Be sure you understand the features, benefits, costs and fees associated with any annuity product before you invest.

6

HOW TO GET THROUGH THE RETIREMENT RED ZONE

In the game of football, the area from the 20-yard line to the goal line is known as the red zone. When you're in this zone, the field is getting smaller. The pressure is on and the last thing you want to do is "drop the ball". The most successful football teams are the ones who are good at scoring touchdowns when in this red zone. This red zone is also an apt analogy for the critical period during which you transition out of the accumulation phase and into the distribution phase of investing.

The red zone of your retirement is the five years prior to and the five years just after retiring. To fail when in the retirement red zone means a significant loss of money, which then cripples your ability to earn returns and maintain a durable source of income throughout your lifetime. The playing field, or number of years left to grow your money, has been significantly shortened, which means that losing money during the red zone years can exponentially increase your chances of running out of money.

Early on in your career and even later on during your accumulation years, you have more time to utilize an accumulation strategy. You must be aware of the danger zone that occurs during that ten-year window as a retiree. To understand exactly why this is such a critical time, we're going to talk about the **Math of Rebounds** and the **Sequence of Returns**.

RECOVERING FROM LOSS

A fickle market can raise the eyebrows of even the most veteran investor. Taking a hit in the market hurts no matter how stable your income. Part of the pain comes from knowing that when you take a step back in the market, it requires an even larger step forward to return to where you were. As the market goes up and down, those larger gains you need to realize to get back to zero start to look even more daunting. Most people don't realize, however, that when you take a 50 percent loss, it takes more than a 50 percent gain to get back to even again. To simplify this *Math of Rebounds*, as it is sometimes called, let's do the math using a simple dollar bill:

If you have a dollar and you lose 50 percent, you have 50 cents left. Now let's say that investment goes up by 50 percent. Now you have 75 cents, and your investment has gone up by 50 percent and down by 50 percent. Your account statement would register this as an average return of 0, but that's not what it looks like to you in terms of real money. You just lost 25 percent, which means you lost money.

THE SEQUENCE OF RETURNS

What happens when you don't secure your income needs first and a loss occurs? Your account value drops, and if this drop happens during the red zone period, your ability to earn sustainable returns is permanently compromised. Additionally, the loss is further compounded by your continued withdrawals.

The following visual can help you better understand this phenomenon known as *the Sequence of Returns or Sequence Risk.*

Sequence Risk

☆ ☆ ☆ ☆ ☆

Starting principal: $500,000
Income: 5% of first-year principal
Inflation: 3%

If you averaged **8.43%** return over 20 years, does the sequence of the gains and losses matter?

The only difference is the order of returns is reversed!

Sequence Risk is real, and you should be aware of it!

Age	Annual Return	Portfolio A Year End Balance	Annual Return	Portfolio B Year End Balance
66	32%	633,450	-37%	290,000
67	-3%	588,000	5%	280,171
68	30%	740,841	16%	298,025
69	8%	769,759	5%	285,343
70	10%	819,213	11%	288,250
71	1%	801,045	29%	341,938
72	38%	1,072,127	-22%	235,519
73	23%	1,287,663	-12%	177,673
74	33%	1,685,358	9%	129,818
75	29%	2,134,671	21%	124,513
76	21%	2,550,208	29%	176,500
77	-9%	2,283,278	33%	134,095
78	-12%	1,976,531	33%	129,239
79	-22%	1,502,887	38%	141,094
80	22%	1,896,101	1%	105,142
81	11%	2,063,447	10%	76,791
82	5%	2,123,645	8%	42,524
83	16%	2,419,867	30%	14,160
84	9%	2,610,357	-3%	0
85	-37%	1,537,562	32%	0

Notice how both investors above start with the exact same account balance of $500,000. They both withdraw 5 percent income from that principal amount, and they both average an 8.43 percent rate of return over the same 20 years. **The only difference is the order in which those returns are calculated.**

Portfolio A sustains a large loss at the **end** of the 20-year period whereas Portfolio B incurs the loss at the **beginning** of retirement during the critical red zone years. Investor B has an account balance of over $1 million dollars at the end of the 20-year period, whereas investor A will run out of money by the age of 84.

What sequence risk shows us is that you can do everything right, work hard, and save money in a nice big fat 401(k), but if you are one of the unlucky souls who happen to retire during a bad year and the market goes down when you are in the red zone, that loss will inevitably change what the future of your retirement looks like.

RETIREMENT AND THE HAIL MARY PASS

For anyone not familiar with the game of football, when the losing team has the ball and there's not much time to score and they are too far away to earn yardage by the usual means, they do what's called a Hail Mary pass. They send a bunch of receivers down the field, throw the ball up in the air and hope that somebody will catch it for a touchdown. These passes usually don't work, but every once in a while they do.

While catching a Hail Mary pass can be a great moment in a game, it's not how you want to play the final quarter of your life. You don't want to be scrambling around, hoping and praying and throwing that nest egg as far as it can go in hopes that someone or something will catch it. For the investor who hasn't saved enough money or who lost money and is shooting for large returns, staying in the stock market during the distribution years can feel like an act of desperation. When you are managing your money by yourself, emotions inevitably enter into the mix. The Dow Jones Industrial Average and the S&P 500 represent more to you than market fluctuations. They represent a portion of your retirement. It's hard not to be emotional about it.

Everyone knows you should buy low and sell high. But this is what is more likely to happen:

The market takes a downturn, similar to the 2008 crash, and investors see as much as a 30 percent loss in their stock holdings. It's hard to watch, and it's harder to bear the pain of losing that much money. The math of rebounds means that they will need to rely on even larger gains just to get back to where things were before the downturn. They sell. But eventually, and inevitably, the market begins to rise again. Maybe slowly, maybe with some moderate growth, but by the time the average investor notices an upward trend and wants to buy in again, they have already missed a great deal of the gains.

>> *Maggie's situation illustrates how market volatility can have major repercussions for an individual investor. Maggie works for Acme Paper Company for 34 years. During her time there, she acquires bonuses and pay raises that often include shares of stock in the company. She also dedicates part of her paycheck every month to a 401(k) that bought Acme stock. By the time she retires, Maggie has $250,000 worth of Acme stock.*

Although she had contributes to her 401(k) account every month, Maggie doesn't cultivate any other assets that could generate income for her during retirement. Maggie also retires early at age 62 because of her failing health. The commute to work every day was becoming difficult in her weakened condition and she wanted to enjoy the rest of her life in retirement instead of working at Acme.

Because she retires early, Maggie fails to maximize her Social Security benefit. While she lives a modest lifestyle, her income needs will still be $3,500 per month. Maggie's monthly Social Security check will only cover $1,900, leaving her with a $1,600 income gap. To supplement her Social Security check, Maggie sells $1,600 of her Acme stock each month to meet her income needs. A $250,000 401(k) is *nothing to sneeze at, but reducing its value by $1,600 every month will barely last Maggie 10 years. And that's if the market stays neutral or grows modestly. If the market takes a downturn, the money that Maggie relied on to fill her income gap will rapidly diminish. Even if the market starts going up in a couple of years, it will take much larger gains for her to recover the value that she lost.*

Unhappily for Maggie, she retired in 2007, just before the major market downturn that lasted for several years. She lost more than 20 percent of the value of her stock. Because Maggie needed to sell her stock to meet her basic income needs, the market price of the stock was secondary to her need for the money. When she needed money, she was forced to sell however many shares she needed to fill her income gap that month. And if she has a financial crisis, involving her need for medical care, for example, she will be forced to sell stock even if the market is low and her shares are nearly worthless.

Maggie realizes that she could have relied on an investment structured to deliver her a regular income while protecting the value of her investment. She could have kept her $250,000 from diminishing while enjoying her lifestyle into retirement regardless of the volatility of the market. Ideally, Maggie would have restructured her 401(k) to reflect the level of risk that she was able to take. In her case, she would have had most of her money in Green Money assets, allowing her to rely on the value of her assets when she needed them.

A LOOK AT THE DALBAR STUDY

In 2013, DALBAR, the well-respected financial services market research firm, released their annual "Quantitative Analysis of Investment Behavior" report (QAIB). The report studied the impact of market volatility on individual investors: a person like Maggie,

or anyone who was managing (or mismanaging) their own investments in the stock market.

According to the study, volatility not only caused investors
to make decisions based on their emotions, those decisions also
harmed their investments and prevented them from realizing
potential gains. So why do people meddle so much with their
investments when the market is fluctuating? Part of the reason
is that many people have financial obligations that they don't
have control over. Significant expenses like house payments, the
unexpected cost of replacing a broken-down car, and medical bills
can put people in a position where they need money. If they need
to sell investments to come up with that money, they don't have
the luxury of selling when they *want* to. They must sell when they
need to.

DALBAR's "Quantitative Analysis of Investor Behavior" has
been used to measure the effects of investors' buying, selling and
mutual fund switching decisions since 1994. The QAIB shows
time and time again over nearly a 20-year period that the average
investor earns less, and in many cases, significantly less than the
performance of mutual funds suggests. QAIB's goal is to improve
independent investor performance and to help financial professionals provide helpful advice and investment strategies that address the concerns and behaviors of the average investor.

An excerpt from the report claims that:*

*"QAIB offers guidance on how and where investor behaviors can be
improved. No matter what the state of the mutual fund industry,
boom or bust: Investment results are more dependent on investor
behavior than on fund performance. Mutual fund investors who hold
on to their investments are more successful than those who time the
market.*

---

*2013 QAIB, Dalbar, March 2013

QAIB uses data from the Investment Company Institute (ICI), Standard & Poor's and Barclays Capital Index Products to compare mutual fund investor returns to an appropriate set of benchmarks.
There are actually three primary causes for the chronic shortfall for both equity and fixed income investors:
  1. Capital not available to invest. This accounts for 25 percent to 35 percent of the shortfall.
  2. Capital needed for other purposes. This accounts for 35 percent to 45 percent of the shortfall.
  3. Psychological factors. These account for 45 percent to 55 percent of the shortfall."

The key findings of Dalbar's QAIB report provide compelling statistics about how individual investment strategies produced negative outcomes for the majority of investors:
  • Psychological factors account for 45 percent to 55 percent of the chronic investment return shortfall for both equity and fixed income investors.
  • Asset allocation is designed to handle the investment decision-making for the investor, which can materially reduce the shortfall due to psychological factors.
  • Successful asset allocation investing requires investors to act on two critical imperatives:
    1. Balance capital preservation and appreciation so that they are aligned with the investor's objective.
    2. Select a qualified allocator.
  • The best way for an investor to determine their risk tolerance is to utilize a risk tolerance assessment. However, these assessments must be accessible and usable.
  • Evaluating allocator quality requires analysis of the allocator's underlying investments, decision making process and whether or not past efforts have produced successful outcomes.

- Choosing a top allocator makes a significant difference in the investment results one will achieve.
- Mutual fund retention rates suggest that the average investor has not remained invested for long enough periods to derive the potential benefits of the investment markets.
- Retention rates for asset allocation funds exceed those of equity and fixed income funds by over a year.
- Investors' ability to correctly time the market is highly dependent on the direction of the market. Investors generally guess right more often in up markets. However, in 2012 investors guessed right only 42 percent of the time during a bull market.
- Analysis of investor fund flows compared to market performance further supports the argument that investors are unsuccessful at timing the market. Market upswings rarely coincide with mutual fund inflows while market downturns do not coincide with mutual fund outflows.
- Average equity mutual fund investors gained 15.56 percent compared to a gain of 15.98 percent that just holding the S&P 500 produced.
- The shortfall in the long-term annualized return of the average mutual fund equity investor and the S&P 500 continued to decrease in 2012.
- The fixed-income investor experienced a return of 4.68 percent compared to an advance of 4.21 percent on the Barclays Aggregate Bond Index.
- The average fixed income investor has failed to keep up with inflation in nine out of the last 14 years.*

It doesn't take financial services market research report to tell you that market volatility is out of your control. The report does prove,

---

2013 QAIB, Dalbar, March 2013

however, that before you experience market volatility, you should have an investment plan, and when the market is fluctuating, you should stand by your investment plan. You should also review and discuss your investment plan with your financial professional on a regular basis, ensuring he/she is aware of any changes in your goals, financial circumstances, your health or your risk tolerance. When the economy is under stress and the markets are volatile, investors can feel vulnerable. That vulnerability causes people to tinker with their portfolios in an attempt to outsmart the market. Financial professionals, however, don't try to time the market for their clients. They try to tap into the gains that can be realized by committing to long-term investment strategies.

CHAPTER 6 RECAP //

- The *Red Zone* during retirement is the five years just prior to retirement and the five years just after you retire and begin taking distributions.

- The timing of market downturns is more critical to retirees than to the average investor. If you are making withdrawals on a market investment without first protecting your income, and the account suffers a loss, rapid depletion of your funds will change what the future of your retirement looks like.

- The *Math of Rebounds* shows us that you have to do more than just earn back your initial loss in order to get back to where you were before. Use the percentage of the investment and not dollar amount to calculate what you need to earn in order to recapture your losses.

- The *Sequence of Returns* shows us that once you enter into your distribution years, it is the order of the returns that matters more than the actual rate of return.

- Emotions inevitably enter the mix during stock market downturns. According to the DALBAR "Quantitative Analysis of Investment Behavior" report released in 2013, the average fixed income investor managing their money alone failed to keep up with inflation in nine out of the last 14 years.

7

WHAT IS YELLOW
MONEY?

Now that you've calculated the Rule of 100, determined how much risk you have and how much you want, and you've determined how much Green Money you need to meet your short-term and mid-term income needs, it's time to look at what you have left. The money you have left after you've calculated your Green Money needs has the potential of becoming Red Money: your stocks, mutual funds and other investment products that you want to continue accumulating value with the market. You now have the luxury of taking a closer second look at your Red Money to determine how you would like to manage it.

As you read earlier in the key findings of the DALBAR report, the deck is stacked against the individual investor. Remember that the average investor on a fixed income failed to keep pace with inflation in nine of the last 14 years, meaning the inherent risk in managing your Red Money is very real and could have a lasting impact on your assets. So, how much of your Red Money do you invest, and in what kinds of markets, investment products and stocks do you invest? There are a lot of different directions in which you can take your Red Money. One thing is for sure: significant accumulation depends on investing in the market. How you go about doing it is different for everyone. Gathering stocks, bonds and investment funds together in a portfolio without a cohesive strategy behind them could cause you to miss out on the benefits of a more thoughtful and planful approach. The end result is that you may never really understand what your money is doing, where and how it is really invested, and which investment principles are behind the investment products you hold. While you may have goals for each individual piece of your portfolio, it is likely that you don't have a comprehensive plan for your Red Money, which may mean that *you are taking on more risk than you would like, and are getting less return for it than is possible.*

Enter **Yellow Money.** Yellow Money is money that is managed by a professional *with a purpose.* After your income needs are met and you have assets that you would like to dedicate to accumulation, there are decisions you need to make about how to invest those assets. You can buy stocks, index funds, mutual funds, bonds—you name it—you can invest in it. However, the difference between Red Money and Yellow Money is that Yellow Money has a cohesive strategy behind it that is *implemented by a professional.* When you manage your Red Money with an investment plan, it becomes Yellow Money: *money that is being managed with a specific purpose, a specific set of focused goals and a specific strategy in mind.* Yellow Money is still a type of Red Money. It comes with different levels of risk. But Yellow Money is under the watchful eye of professionals who have a stake in the success of your money in the market and who can recommend a range of strategies from those designed for preservation to those targeting rapid growth. You don't want to miss out on achieving the right level of risk, and more importantly, composing a careful plan for the return of your assets.

It can be helpful to think of Red Money and Yellow Money with this analogy:

If you needed to travel through an unfamiliar city in a foreign country, you could rent a car or perhaps hire a driver. Were you to drive yourself, you would try to gain guidance from perplexing road signs and need to adhere to traffic rules—with no experience or assistance to lean on. It would take longer to get to where you want to go, and the chance of a traffic accident would be higher. If you hired a driver, they would manage your journey. A driver would know the route, how to avoid traffic, and follow the rules of the road.

Red Money is like driving yourself. With Yellow Money, you are still traveling by car, but now you have a professional working on your behalf.

TAKING A CLOSER LOOK AT YOUR PORTFOLIO

Think about your investment portfolio. Think specifically of what you would consider your Red Money. Do you know what is there? You may have several different investment products like individual mutual funds, bond accounts, stocks, etc. You may have inherited a stock portfolio from a relative, or you might be invested in a bond account offered by the company for which you worked due to your familiarity with them. While you may or may not be managing your investments individually, the reality is that you probably don't have an overall management strategy for all of your investments. Investments that aren't managed are simply Red Money, or money that is at risk in the market.

Harnessing the earning potential of your Red Money relies on more than a collection of stocks and bonds, however. It needs guided management. A good Yellow Money manager uses the knowledge they have about the level of risk with which you are comfortable, what you need or want to use your money for, when you want or need it and how you want to use it. The Yellow Money objects that they choose for you will still have a certain level of risk, but under the right management, control and process, you have a far better chance of a successful outcome that meets your specific needs.

When you sit down with an investment professional, you can look at all of your assets together. Chances are that you have accumulated a number of different assets over the last 20, 30 or 50 years. You may have a 401(k), an IRA, a Roth IRA, an account of self-directed stocks, a brokerage account, etc. Wherever you put your money, a financial professional will go through your assets and help you determine the level of risk to which you are exposed now and should be exposed in the future.

Here is a typical example of how an investment professional can be helpful to a future retiree with Yellow Money needs:

> » Samantha is 65 years old and wants to retire in two years. She has a 401(k) from her job to which she has contributed for 26 years. She also has some stocks that her late husband managed. Samantha also has $55,000 in a mutual fund that her sister recommended to her five years ago and $30,000 in another mutual fund that she heard about at work. She takes a look at her assets one day and decides that she doesn't understand what they add up to or what kind of retirement they will provide. She decides to meet with an investment professional. Samantha's professional immediately asks her:
>
> **1. Does she know exactly where all of her money is?** Samantha doesn't know much about all her husband's stocks, which have now become hers. Their value is at $100,000

invested in three large cap companies. Samantha is unsure of the companies and whether she should hold or sell them.

2. Does she know what types of assets she owns? *Yes and no. She knows she had a 401(k) and IRAs, but she is unfamiliar with her husband's self-directed stock portfolio or the type of mutual funds she owns. Furthermore she is unclear as to how to manage the holdings as she nears retirement.*

3. Does she know the strategies behind each one of the investment products she owns? *While Samantha knows she had a 401(k), an IRA and mutual fund holdings, she doesn't know how her 401(k) is organized or how to make it more conservative as she nears retirement. She is unsure whether her IRA is a Roth or traditional variety and how to draw income from them? She really does not have specific investment principles guiding her investment decisions, and she doesn't know anything about her husband's individual stocks. One major concern for Samantha is whether her family would be okay if she were not around?*

After determining Samantha's assets, her financial professional prepares a consolidated report that lays out all of her assets for her to review. Her professional explains each one of them to her. Samantha discovers that although she is two years away from retiring, her 401(k) is organized with an amount of risk with which she is not comfortable. Sixty percent of her 401(k) is at risk, far off the mark if we abide by the Rule of 100. Samantha opts to be more conservative than the Rule of 100 suggests, as she will rely on her 401(k) for most of her immediate income needs after retirement. Samantha's professional also points out several instances of overlap between her mutual funds. Samantha learns that while she is comfortable with one of her mutual funds, she does not agree with the management principles of the other. In the end, Samantha's professional helps her re-organize her 401(k) to secure her more Green Money for retirement income. Her professional also uses her mutual fund and her husband's stock assets to create a growth oriented investment plan that Samantha will rely on for Need Later Money in 15 years when she plans on relocating closer to her children and grandchildren. By creating an overall investment strategy, Samantha is able to meet her targeted goals in retirement. Samantha's financial professional worked closely with her and her tax professional to minimize the tax impact of any asset sales on Samantha's situation.

Like Samantha, you may have several savings vehicles: a 401(k), an IRA to which you regularly contribute, some mutual funds to which you make monthly contributions, etc. But what is your *overall investment strategy?* Do you have one in place? Do you want one that will help you meet your retirement goals? Yellow Money looks at *ALL* your accounts and all their different strategies to create a plan that helps them all work together. Your current investment situation may not reflect your wishes. As a matter of fact, it likely doesn't.

You may have a better understanding of your assets than Samantha did, but even someone with an investment strategy can benefit from having a financial professional review their portfolio:

» Frank is 69 years old. He retired four years ago. He relied on income from an IRA for three years in order to increase his Social Security benefit. He also made significant investments in 36 different mutual funds. He chose to diversify among the funds by selecting a portion for growth, another for good dividends, another that focused on promising small cap companies and a final portion that work like index funds. All the money that Frank had in mutual funds he considered Need Later Money that he wanted to rely on in his 80s. After the

stock market took a hit in 2008, Frank lost some confidence in his investments and decided to sit down with a financial professional to see if his portfolio was able to recover.

The professional Frank met with was able to determine what goals he had in mind. Specifically, the financial professional determined what Frank actually wanted and needed the money for, and when he needed it. His professional also looked inside each of the mutual funds and discovered several instances of overlap. While Frank had created diversity in his portfolio by selecting funds focused on different goals, he didn't account for overlap in the companies in which the funds were invested. Out of the 36 funds, his professional found that 20 owned nearly identical stock. While most of the companies were good investments, the high instance of overlap did not contribute to the healthy investment diversity that Frank wanted. Frank's financial professional also provided him with a report that explained the concentration ratio of his holdings (noting how much of his portfolio was contained within the top 25 stock holdings), the percentage of his portfolio that each company in which he invested in represented (showing the percentage of net assets that each company made up as an overall position in his portfolio) and the portfolio date of his account (showing when the funds in his portfolio were last updated: as funds are required to report updates only twice per year, it was possible that some of his fund reports could be six months old).

Frank's professional consolidated his assets into one investment management strategy. This allowed Frank's investments to be managed by someone he trusted who knew his specific investment goals and needs. Eliminating redundancy and overlap in his portfolio was easy to do but difficult to detect since Frank had multiple funds with multiple brokerage firms. Frank sat down with a professional to see if his mutual funds could perform well, and he left with a consolidated management plan and a money manager that understood him personally. That's Yellow Money at its best.

AVOIDING EMOTIONAL INVESTING

There's no way around it; people get emotional about their money. And for good reason. You've spent your life working for it, exchanging your time and talent for it, and making decisions about how to invest it, save it and make it grow. The maintenance of your lifestyle and your plans for retirement all depend on it. The best investment strategies, however, don't rely on emotions. One of Yellow Money's greatest strengths lies in the fact that it is managed by someone who understands your needs and desires, but doesn't make decisions about your money under the influence of emotion.

A well-managed investment account meets your goals as a whole, not in individualized and piecemeal ways. Professional money managers do this by creating requirements for each type of investment in which they put your money. We'll call them "screens." Your money manager will run your holdings through the screens they have created to evaluate different types of investment strategies. A professionally managed account will only have holdings that meet the requirements laid out in the overall management plan that was designed to meet your investment goals. The holdings that don't make it through the screens, the ones that don't contribute to your investment goals, are sold and redistributed to investments that your financial professional has determined to be appropriate.

Different screens apply to different Yellow Money strategies. For example, if one of your goals is significant growth, which would require taking on more risk alongside the potential for more return, an investment professional would screen for companies that have high rates of revenue and sales growth, high earnings growth, rising profit margins, and innovative products. On the other hand, if you want your portfolio to be used for income, which would call for lower risk and less return, your professional would screen for dividend yield and sector diversification. *Every investor has a different goal, and every goal requires a customized strategy that uses quantitative screens.* A professional will create a portfolio that reflects your investment desires. If some of the current assets you own complement the strategies that your professional recommends, those will likely stay in your portfolio.

Screening your assets removes emotions from the equation. It removes attachment to underperforming or overly risky investments. Financial professionals aren't married to particular stocks or mutual funds for any reason. They go by the numbers and see your portfolio through a lens shaped by your retirement goals. Your professional understands your wants and needs, and creates an investment strategy that takes your life events and future plans into account. It's a planful approach, and it allows you to tap into the tools and resources of a professional who has built a career around successful investing. Managing money is a full-time job and is best left to a professional money manager.

Removing emotions from investing also allows you to be unaffected by the day-to-day volatility of the market. Your financial professional doesn't ask where the market is going to be in a year, three years or a month from now. If you look at the value of the stock market from the beginning of the twentieth century to today, it's going up. Despite the Great Depression, despite the 1987 crash, despite the 2008 market downturn, the market, as a whole, trends up. Remember the major market downturn in 2008 when the market lost 30 percent of its value? Not only did it completely recover, it has far exceeded its 2008 value. Emotional investing led countless people to sell low as the market went down, and buy the same shares back when the market started to recover. That's an expensive way to do business. While you can't afford to lose money that you need in two, three or five years, your Need Later Money has time to grow. The best way to do so is to make it Yellow.

CREATING AN INVESTMENT STRATEGY

Just like Samantha and Frank, chances are that you can benefit from taking a more managed investment approach tailored to your goals. Yellow Money is generally Need Later Money that you want to grow for needs you'll have in at least 10 years. You can work with your financial planner to create investments that meet your needs within different timeframes. You may need to rely on some of your Yellow Money in 10, 15 or 20 years, whether for additional income, a large purchase you plan on making or a vacation. Whatever you want it for, you will need it down the road. A financial professional can help you rescale the risk of your assets as they grow, helping you lock in your profits and secure a source of income you can depend on later.

So what does a Yellow Money account look like? Here's what it *doesn't* look like: a portfolio with 49 small cap mutual funds, a dozen individual stocks and an assortment of bond accounts. A brokerage account with a hodgepodge of investments, even if goal-oriented, is not a professionally managed account. It's still Red Money. Remember, Yellow Money is a managed account that has an overarching investment philosophy. When you look at making investments that will perform to meet your future income needs, the burning question becomes: How much should you have in the market and how should it be invested? Working with a professional will help you determine how much risk you should take, how to balance your assets so they will meet your goals and how to plan for the big ticket items, like health care expenses, that may be in your future. Yes, Yellow Money is exposed to risk, but by working with a professional, you can manage that risk in a productive way.

WHY YELLOW MONEY?

If you have met your immediate income needs for retirement, why bother with professionally managing your other assets? The money you have accumulated above and beyond your income needs probably has a greater purpose. It may be for your children or grandchildren. You may want to give money to a charity or organization that you admire. In short, you may want to craft your legacy. It would be advantageous to grow your assets in the best manner possible. A financial professional has built a career around managing money in profitable ways. They are experts under the supervision of the organization that they represent.

Turning to Yellow Money also means that you don't have to burden yourself with the time commitment, the stress, and the cost of determining how to manage your money. Yellow Money can help you better enjoy your retirement. Do you want to sit down in your home office every day and determine how to best allocate your assets, or do you want to be living your life while someone else manages your money for you? When a financial professional manages the majority of your Red Money with a specific purpose, you don't have to be worrying about which stocks to buy and sell today or tomorrow.

SEEKING FINANCIAL ADVICE: STOCK BROKERS VS. INVESTMENT ADVISOR REPRESENTATIVES

Investors basically have access to two types of advice in today's financial world: advice from stockbrokers and advice given by investment advisors. Most investors, however, don't know the difference between types of advice and the people from whom they receive advice. Today, there are two primary types of advice offered to investors: advice given by a commission-based registered representative (brokers) and advice given by fee-based Investment Advisor Representatives. Unfortunately, many investors are not aware that a difference exists; nor have they been explained the

distinction between the two types of advice. In a survey taken by TD Ameritrade, the top reasons investors choose to work with an independent registered investment advisor are:*
- Registered Investment Advisors are required, as fiduciaries, to offer advice that is in the best interest of clients
- More personalized service and competitive fee structure offered at a Registered Investment Advisor firm
- Dissatisfaction with full commission brokers

The truth is that there is a great deal of difference between stockbrokers and investment advisor representatives. For starters, investment advisor representatives are obligated to act in an investor's best interests in every all aspect of a financial relationship. Confusion continues to exist among investors struggling to find the best financial advice out there and the most credible sources of advice.

Here is some information to help clear up the confusion so you can find good advice from a professional you can trust:
- Investment advisor representatives have the fiduciary duty to act in a client's best interest at all times with every investment decision they make. Stockbrokers and brokerage firms usually do not act as fiduciaries to their investors and are not obligated to make decisions that are entirely in the best interest of their customers. For example, if you decide you want to invest in precious metals, a stockbroker would offer you a precious metals account from their firm. An Investment Advisor would find you a precious metals account that is the best fit for you based on the investment strategy of your portfolio.
- Investment advisors give their clients a Form ADV describing the methods that the professional uses to do busi-

ness. An Investment Advisor also obtains client consent regarding any conflicts of interest that could exist with the business of the professional.

- Stock brokers and brokerage firms are not obligated to provide comparable types of disclosure to their customers.

- Whereas stock brokers and firms routinely earn large profits by trading as principal with customers, Investment Advisors cannot trade with clients as principal (except in very limited and specific circumstances).

- Investment Advisors charge a pre-negotiated fee with their clients in advance of any transactions. They cannot earn additional profits or commissions from their customers' investments without prior consent. Registered Investment Advisors are commonly paid an asset-based fee that aligns their interests with those of their clients. Brokerage firms and stockbrokers, on the other hand, have much different payment agreements. Their revenues may increase regardless of the performance of their customers' assets.

- Unlike brokerage firms, where investment banking and underwriting are commonplace, Registered Investment Advisors must manage money in the best interests of their customers. Because Registered Investment Advisors charge set fees for their services, their focus is on their client. Brokerage firms may focus on other aspects of the firm that do not contribute to the improvement of their clients' assets.

- Unlike brokers, Registered Investment Advisors do not get commissions from fund or insurance companies for selling their investment products.

Just to drive home the point, here is what a fiduciary duty to a client means for a Registered Investment Advisor. Registered Investment Advisors must:*

- Always act in the best interest of their client and make investment decisions that reflect their goals.
- Identify and monitor securities that are illiquid.
- When appropriate, employ fair market valuation procedures.
- Observe procedures regarding the allocation of investment opportunities, including new issues and the aggregation of orders.
- Have policies regarding affiliated broker-dealers and maintenance of brokerage accounts.
- Disclose all conflicts of interest.
- Have policies on use of brokerage commissions for research.
- Have policies regarding directed brokerage, including step-out trades and payment for order flow.
- Abide by a code of ethics.

---

* *2011 Advisor Sentiment Study,* commissioned by *TD AMERITRADE. TD Ameritrade, Inc.*

CHAPTER 7 RECAP //

- Yellow Money is money that is managed by a professional. It is still considered a type of Red Money, but the risk is managed. There is a dedicated direction, strategy and end goal in mind, which makes it less dangerous.
- Red Money is like driving yourself in unfamiliar territory. With Yellow Money, you are still traveling by car, but now you have a professional driving on your behalf.
- Yellow Money is managed without emotions. A financial professional qualified to manage money uses a specific criteria designed to fit your overall financial plan so that it works the way you want it to.

8

LIQUIDITY, SAFETY AND RETURN:
A PLAY-BY-PLAY

Earlier, we discussed how today's investment options require advice that is relevant to today. Traditional, outdated investment strategies are not only ineffective, they can be harmful to the average investor. One of the most traditional ways of thinking about investing is the risk versus reward trade-off. It goes something like this:

Investment options that are considered safer carry less risk, but also offer the potential for less return.

Riskier investment options carry the burden of volatility and a greater potential for loss, but they also offer a greater potential for large rewards.

Most professionals move their clients back and forth along this range, shifting between investments that are safer and investments that are structured for growth. Essentially, the old rules of investing dictate that you can either choose relative safety *or* return, but you can't have both.

Updated investment strategies work with the flexibility of liquidity to remake the rules for our playbook. Here is how:

There are three dimensions that are inherent in any investment: *Liquidity, Safety,* and *Return.* You can maximize any two of these dimensions at the expense of the third. If you choose Safety and Liquidity, this is like keeping your assets in a checking account or savings account. This option delivers a lot of Safety and Liquidity, but at the expense of any Return. On the other hand, if you choose Liquidity and Return, meaning you have the potential for great return and can still reclaim your money whenever you choose, you will likely be exposed to a very high level of risk.

Understanding Liquidity can help you break the old Risk versus Safety trade-off. By identifying assets from which you don't require Liquidity, you can place yourself in a position to potentially profit from relatively safe investments that provide a higher than average rate of return.

Choosing Safety and Return over Liquidity can have significant impacts on the accumulation of your assets. In Harold's case, the paradigm shift from earning and saving to leveraging assets was a costly one.

» *Harold is a corn and soybean farmer with 1,200 acres of land. He routinely retains somewhere between $40,000 and $80,000 in his checking and savings accounts. If a major piece of equipment fails and needs repair or replacement, Harold will need the money available to pay for the equipment and carry on with farming. If the price of feed for his cattle goes up one year, he will need to compensate for* *the increased overhead to his farming operation. He isn't a particularly wealthy farmer, but he has little choice but to keep a portion of money on hand in case something comes up and he must access it quickly. Most of his capital is held in livestock in the pasture or crops in the ground tied up for six to eight months of the year. When a major financial need arises, Harold can't just harvest 10 acres of soybeans and use them for payment. He needs to depend heavily on Liquidity in order to be a successful farmer.*

Old habits die hard, however, and when Harold finally hangs up his overalls and quits farming, he keeps his bank accounts flush with cash, just like in the old days. After selling the farm and the equipment, Harold keeps a huge portion of the profits in Liquid investments because that's what he is familiar with. Unfortunately for Harold, with his pile of money sitting in his checking account, he isn't even keeping pace with inflation. After all his hard work as a farmer, his money is losing value every day because he didn't shift to a paradigm of leveraging his assets to generate income and accumulate value.

Almost anything would be a better option for Harold than clinging to Liquidity. He could have done something better to get either more return from his money or more safety, and at the very least would not have lost out to inflation.

As you can see, choosing Liquidity solely can be a costly option. The sooner you want your money back, the less you can leverage it for Safety or Return. If you have the option of putting your money in a long-term investment, you will be sacrificing Liquidity, but potentially gaining both Safety and Return. Rethinking your approach to money in this way can make a world of difference and can provide you with a structured way to generate income while allowing the value of your asset to grow over time.

YOUR RAINY DAY FUND

The establishment of an emergency fund is key to achieving a successful balance of safety, liquidity, and return. Liquidity is the most essential component of this play, because you want to be able to access this money quickly and easily. When your roof needs repairs or the water heater quits or some other financial need appears, you want to know from where to pull the funds. Taking the money from a qualified account can trigger a tax event; pulling the money from your income producing assets could cause a shortfall down the road. Having the money in a safe, liquid account isn't fancy or sexy, but it means you can rest easy knowing that no matter what curve ball life throws your way, you're covered.

How much do you need to have in your rainy day fund? The dollar amount of your emergency fund will depend on your goals and your existing situation. Working with a financial professional held to fiduciary standards can help you get clarity about the amount you need.

Think about it. If you haven't sat down and created an income plan for your retirement, your perceived need for Liquidity is a guess. You don't know how much cash you'll need to fill the income gap if you don't know the amount of your Social Security benefit or the total of your other income options. If you *have* determined your income need and made a plan for filling your income gap, you can partition your assets based on when you will need them. With an income plan in place, *you can use new rules to enjoy both Safety and Return from your assets.*

CHAPTER 8 RECAP //

- The three aspects of any investment include liquidity, safety, and return. You can choose to maximize any two against the third.
- Choosing to maximize liquidity alone can be an expensive option because the sooner you need your money back, the less you can leverage it for safety and return. To plan for a successful retirement in today's economy requires a creative use of today's financial tools.
- A comprehensive income plan during retirement should include provisions for a rainy day fund. This fund should be a safe, liquid account you can readily access.

9

TAXES AND RETIREMENT

Taxes play an important role in the playbook of retirement planning. Everyone is familiar with taxes (you've been paying them your entire working life), but not everyone is familiar with how to make tax planning a part of their retirement strategy.

Taxes are taxes, right? You'll pay them before retirement and you'll pay them during retirement. What's the difference? The truth is that a planful approach to taxes can help you save money, protect your assets and ensure that your legacy remains intact.

How can a tax form do all that? The answer lies in planning. *Tax planning* and *tax reporting* are two very different things. Most people only *report* their taxes. March rolls around, people pull out their 1040s or use TurboTax to enter their income and taxable assets, and ship it off to Uncle Sam at the IRS. If you use a CPA to report your taxes, you are essentially paying them to record history. You have the option of being proactive with your taxes and to plan for your future by making smart, informed decisions about how taxes affect your overall financial plan. Working with a financial professional who, along with a CPA, makes recommendations about your finances to you, will keep you looking forward instead of in the rearview mirror as you enter retirement.

TAXES AND RETIREMENT

When you retire, you move from the earning and accumulation phase of your life into the asset distribution phase of your life. For most people, that means relying on Social Security, a 401(k), an IRA, or a pension. Wherever you have put your Green Money for retirement, you are going to start relying on it to provide you with the income that once came as a paycheck. Most of these distributions will be considered income by the IRS and will be taxed as such. There are exceptions to that (not all of your Social Security income is taxed, and income from Roth IRAs is not taxed), but for the most part, your distributions will be subject to income taxes.

Regarding assets that you have in an IRA or a 401(k) plan , when you reach 70 ½ years of age, you will be required to draw a certain amount of money from your IRA as income each year. That amount depends on your age and the balance in your IRA. The amount that you are required to withdraw as income is called a Required Minimum Distribution (RMD). Why are you required to withdraw money from your own account? Chances are the money in that account has grown over time, and the government wants to collect taxes on that growth. If you have a large balance in an IRA, there's a chance your RMD could increase your income significantly enough to put you into a higher tax bracket, subjecting you to a higher tax rate.

Here's where tax planning can really begin to work strongly in your favor. In the distribution phase of your life, you have a predictable income based on your RMDs, your Social Security benefit and any other income-generating assets you may have. What really impacts you at this stage is how much of that money you keep in your pocket after taxes. Essentially, *you will make more money saving on taxes than you will by making more money.* If you can reduce your tax burden by 30, 20 or even 10 percent, you earn yourself that much more money by not paying it in taxes.

How do you save money on taxes? By having a plan. In this instance, a financial professional can work with the CPAs at their firm to create a **distribution plan** that minimizes your taxes and maximizes your annual net income.

BUILDING A TAX DIVERSIFIED PORTFOLIO

So far so good: avoid taxes, maximize your net annual income and have a plan for doing it. When people decide to leverage the experience and resources of a financial professional, they may not be thinking of how distribution planning and tax planning will benefit their portfolios. Often more exciting prospects like planning income annuities, investing in the market and structuring investments for growth rule the day. Taxes, however, play a crucial role in retirement planning. Achieving those tax goals requires knowledge of options, foresight and professional guidance.

Finding the path to a good tax plan isn't always a simple task. Every tax return you file is different from the one before it because things constantly change. Your expenses change. Planned or unplanned purchases occur. Health care costs, medical bills, an inheritance, property purchases, reaching an age where your RMD kicks in or travel, any number of things can affect how much income you report and how many deductions you take each year.

Preparing for the ever-changing landscape of your financial life requires a tax-diversified portfolio that can be leveraged to balance the incomes, expenditures and deductions that affect you each year. A financial professional will work with you to answer questions like these:

- What does your tax landscape look like?
- Do you have a tax-diversified portfolio robust enough to adapt to your needs?
- Do you have a diversity of taxable and non-taxable income planned for your retirement?
- Will you be able to maximize your distributions to take advantage of your deductions when you retire?
- Is your portfolio strong enough and tax-diversified enough to adapt to an ever-changing (and usually increasing) tax code?

» *When Karen returns home after a week in the hospital recovering from a knee replacement, the 77-year-old calls her daughter, sister and brother to let them know she is home and feeling well. She also should have called her CPA. Karen's medical expenses for the procedure, her hospital stay, her medications and the ongoing physical therapy she attended amount to more than $50,000.*

*Currently, Americans can deduct medical expenses that are more than 10 percent of their Adjusted Gross Income (AGI). Karen's AGI is $60,000 the year of her knee replacement, meaning she is able to deduct $45,500 of her medical bills from her taxes that year. Her AGI dictated that she could deduct more than 80 percent of her medical expenses that year. **Karen didn't know this.***

Had she been working with a financial professional who regularly asked her about any changes in her life, her spending, or her expenses (expected or unexpected), Karen could have saved thousands of dollars. Karen can also file an amendment to her tax return to recoup the overpayment. **This scenario presumes permanent laws in effect subsequent to 12/31/16**

This relatively simple example of how tax planning can save you money is just the tip of the iceberg. No one can be expected to know the entire U.S. tax code. But a professional who is working with a team of CPAs and financial professionals have an advantage over the average taxpayer who must start from square one on their own every year. Have you been taking advantage of all the deductions that are available to you?

PROACTIVE TAX PLANNING

The implications of proactive tax planning are far reaching, and are larger than many people realize. Remember, doing your taxes in January, February, March or April means you are writing a history book. Planning your taxes in October, November or December means that you are writing the story as it happens. You can look at all the factors that are at play and make decisions that will impact your tax return *before* you file it.

Realizing that tax planning is an aspect of financial planning is an important leap to make. When you incorporate tax planning into your financial planning strategy, it becomes part of the way you maximize your financial potential. Paying less in taxes means you keep more of your money. Simply put, the more money you keep, the more of it you can leverage as an asset. This kind of planning can affect you at any stage of your life. If you are 40 years old, are you contributing the maximum amount to your 401(k) plan? Are you contributing to a Roth IRA? Are you finding ways to structure the savings you are dedicating to your children's education? Do you have life insurance? Taxes and tax planning affects all of these investment tools. Having a relationship with a professional who works with a CPA can help you build a truly comprehensive financial plan that not only works with your investments, but also shapes your assets to find the most efficient ways to prepare for tax time. There may be years that you could benefit from higher distributions because of the tax bracket that you are in, or there could be years you would benefit from taking less. There may be years when you have a lot of deductions and years you have relatively few. **Adapting your distributions to work in concert with your available deductions** is at the heart of smart tax planning. Professional guidance can bring you to the next level of income distribution, allowing you to remain flexible enough to maximize your tax efficiency. And remember, saving money on taxes makes you more money than making money does.

What you have on paper is important: your assets, savings, investments, which are financial expression of your work and time. It's just as important to know how to get it off the paper in a way that keeps most of it in your pocket. Almost anything that involves financial planning also involves taxes. Annuities, investments, IRAs, 401(k)s, 403(b), and many other investment options will have tax implications. Life also has a way of throwing curveballs. Illness, expensive car repair or replacement, or *any event that has a financial impact on your life will likely have a corresponding tax implication* around which you should adapt your financial plan. Tax planning does just that.

One dollar can end up being less than 25 cents to your heirs.

> » *When Christopher's father passed away, he discovered that he was the beneficiary of his father's $500,000 IRA. Christopher has a wife and a family of four children, and he knew that his father had intended for a large portion of the IRA to go toward funding their college educations.*

After Christopher's father's estate is distributed, Christopher, who is 50 years old and whose two oldest sons are entering college, liquidates the IRA. By doing so, his taxable income for that year puts him in a 39.6 percent tax bracket, immediately reducing the value of the asset to $302,000. An additional 3.8 percent surtax on net investment income further diminishes the funds to $283,000. Liquidating the IRA in effect subjects much of Christopher's regular income to the surtax, as well. At this point, Christopher will be taxed at 43.4 percent.

Christopher's state taxes are an additional 9 percent. Moreover, estate taxes on Christopher's father's assets claim another 22 percent. By the time the IRS is through, Christopher's income from the IRA will be taxed at 75 percent, leaving him with $125,000 of the original $500,000. While it would help contribute to the education of his children, it wouldn't come anywhere near completely paying for it, something the $500,000 could have easily done.

As the above example makes clear, leaving an asset to your beneficiaries can be more complicated than it may seem. In the case of a traditional IRA, after federal, estate and state taxes, the asset could literally diminish to as little as 25 percent of its value.

How does working with a professional help you make smarter tax decisions with your own finances? Any financial professional worth their salt will be working with a firm that has a team of trained tax professionals, including CPAs, who have an intimate knowledge of the tax code and how to adapt a financial plan to it.

Here's another example of how taxes have major implications on asset management:

» *Steve and Sue, a 62-year-old couple, begin working with a financial professional in October. After structuring their assets to reflect their risk tolerance and creating assets that would provide them Green Money income during retirement, they feel good about their situation. They make decisions that allow them to maximize their Social Security benefits, they have plenty of options for filling their income gap, and have begun a safe yet ambitious Yellow Money strategy with their professional. When their professional asks them about their tax plan, they tell him their CPA handled their taxes every year, and did a great job. Their professional says, "I don't mean who does your taxes, I mean, who does your tax planning?" Steve and Sue aren't sure how to respond.*

Their professional brings Steve and Sue's financial plan to the firm's CPA and has her run a tax projection for them. A week later their professional calls them with a tax plan for the year that will save them more than $3,000 on their tax return. The couple is shocked. A simple piece of advice from the CPA based on the numbers revealed that if they paid their estimated taxes before the end of the year, they would be able to itemize it as a deduction, allowing them to save thousands of dollars.

This solution won't work for everyone, and it may not work for Steve and Sue every year. That's not the point. By being proactive with their approach to taxes and using the resources made available by their financial professional, they were able to create a tax plan that saved them money.

YELLOW MONEY AND TAXES

There are also tax implications for the money that you have managed professionally. People with portions of their investment portfolio that are actively traded can particularly benefit from having a proactive tax strategy. Without going into too much detail, for tax purposes there are two kinds of investment money: qualified and non-qualified. Different investment strategies can have different effects on how you are taxed on your investments and the growth of your investments. Some are more beneficial for one kind of investment strategy over another. Determining how to plan for the taxation of non-qualified and qualified investments is fodder for holiday party discussions at accounting firms. While it may not be a stimulating topic for the average investor, you don't have to understand exactly how it works in order to benefit from it.

While there are many differences between qualified and non-qualified investments, the main difference is this: qualified plans are designed to give investors tax benefits by deferring taxation of their growth until they are withdrawn. Non-qualified investments are not eligible for these deferral benefits. As such, non-qualified investments are taxed whenever income is realized from them in the form of growth.

Actively and non-actively traded investments provide a simple example of how to position your investments for the best tax advantage. In an actively traded and managed portfolio, there is a high amount of buying and selling of stocks, bonds, funds, ETFs, etc. If that active portfolio of non-qualified investments does well and makes a 20 percent return one year and you are in the 39.6 percent tax bracket, your net gain from that portfolio is only about 12 percent (39.6 percent tax of the 20 percent gain is roughly 8 percent.) In a passive trading strategy, you can use a qualified investment tool, such as an IRA, to achieve 13, 14 or 15 percent growth (much lower than the actively traded portfolio), but still realize a higher net return because the growth of the qualified investment is not taxed until it is withdrawn.

Does this mean that you have to always rely on a buy and hold strategy in qualified investment tools? Not necessarily. The question is, if you have qualified and non-qualified investments, where do you want to position your actively traded and managed assets? Incorporating a planful approach to positioning your investments for more beneficial taxation can be done many ways, but let's consider one example. Keeping your actively managed investment strategies inside an IRA or some other qualified plan could allow you to realize the higher gains of those investments without paying tax on their growth every year. Your more passively managed funds could then be kept in taxable, non-qualified vehicles and methods, and because you aren't realizing income from them on an annual basis by frequently trading them, they grow sheltered from taxation.

If you are interested in taking advantage of tax strategies that maximize your net income, you need the attentive strategies, experience and knowledge of a professional who can give you options that position you for profit. At the end of the day, what's important to you as the consumer is how much you keep.

ESTATE TAXES

The government doesn't just tax your income from investments while you're alive. They will also dip into your legacy.

While estate taxes aren't as hot of a topic as they were a few years ago, they are still an issue of concern for many people with assets. While taxes may not apply on estates that are less than $5 million, certain states have estate taxes with much lower exclusion ratios. Some are as low as $600,000. Many people may have to pay a state estate tax. One strategy for avoiding those types of taxes is to move assets outside of your estate. That can include gifting them to family or friends, or putting them into an irrevocable trust. Life insurance is another option for protecting your legacy.

CHAPTER 9 RECAP //

- When you report your taxes, you are paying to record history. When you *plan* your taxes with a financial professional, you are proactively finding the best options for your tax return.

- It's important to understand the tax repercussions when tapping into assets from a 401(k) or a traditional IRA for use as an income source. Money that is considered qualified by the federal government must be taxed upon distribution.

- At the age of 70 ½, the federal government requires all IRA participants to take their RMD, or Required Minimum Distribution. Failure to take your RMD can cost you thousands of dollars in taxes and penalty fees.

- Taxes play an important role during your retirement. It's important that you understand your obligations, and the differences between tax-deferred and tax-advantaged advantaged accounts.

- You make more money by saving on taxes than you do by making more money. This simple concept becomes extremely valuable to people in retirement and those living on fixed incomes.

10

THE FUTURE OF
U.S. TAXATION

Although the phrase "nothing is certain except for death and taxes" is most famously attributed to Benjamin Franklin, variations of this saying existed even before the country's first taxes were levied, and these words continue to ring true to this day. However, due to recent upheavals in the American financial landscape, this saying might need to be modified to, "nothing is certain except for death and *increasing* taxes."

In the past 10 years alone, the United States has confronted both a debt ceiling and a fiscal cliff, and the federal debt has continued to grow by unprecedented amounts. With the wellbeing of the economy in jeopardy, legislation regarding debt reduction and tax reform has become a hot button issue. Regardless of which legislation has been, or will be, thrown at the American public, the truth of the matter remains the same: the country's current tax revenues cannot cover its obligations.

If the government wants to keep the lights on, it's going to need more income, which not only means that you can count on being taxed, but also on being taxed at an increasing rate.

DEBT CEILING – CAUSE AND EFFECTS

Since 1960, the debt ceiling has been raised by Congress 78 times. Increasing the debt ceiling is needed because the government keeps maxing out its credit limit, which it has been reliant upon since the beginning of the Industrial Revolution. Essentially, each time the federal government reaches the end of its line of credit, Congress raises the debt ceiling to extend it. This type of poor money management behavior is nothing new for many Americans: many people overuse their credit cards and rack up an impressive amount of debt. However, most people do not have the ability to raise the credit limit on a card once they have maxed it out—unless they can show they have the ability to pay the balance back. The only way to pay a credit line back is by making more money than you're spending. In other words, responsibility and a balanced budget are critical components to repaying a debt.

The federal government keeps finding ways to increase its credit line without also finding ways to proportionally cut its spending. Although some spending cuts have been put in place, they are not large enough to be worthy adversaries of the current debt situation. Consequently, the continual increasing of the debt ceiling has raised more than just the ability of the federal government to go further into debt; it has also raised concerns and fears about the direction in which the economy is heading. As investors' worry about the impact that future investment valuations may have on their personal wealth grows progressively serious, the market continues to swing unpredictably.

The truth of the matter is that raising the debt ceiling is only one part of the equation required to address the country's debt problem—tax reform is the other. If the government wants to try to staunch the flow of its ever-rising debt, then it will need to make more money, and the only way the government makes money is by collecting taxes. Unfortunately, however, the government frequently collects less than it spends: in 2014, the government collected approximately $42 billion less per month than it was spending.*

DEBT AND EARNINGS

Currently, the national debt is increasing at an unprecedented rate, rising to levels never seen before and threatening serious harm to the economy. In October 2004, the national debt was $7.4 trillion**, and by October 2014 it had climbed to $17.9 trillion***, which means the national debt grew 241.9 percent during this 10-year time period or 8.4 percent annually compounded. Since that time, the national debt growth rate has receded significantly and the national gross domestic product (GDP) has increased: in 2014, the annual debt growth rate had fallen to 4.5 percent and the GDP was approximately $17.5 trillion, up from $12.3 trillion in 2004.

However, even in spite of this progress, the gravity of the situation remains severe. At the end of 2011, the national debt level was 95.3 percent of the GDP. Economists believe that a sustainable economy exists at a maximum level of approximately

---

* *Congressional Budget Office projected deficit baseline 2014 - 2024*

** *CBO, An Update to the Budget and Economic Outlook: 2014 - 2024*

*** *US Department of the Treasury's Bureau of the Fiscal Service, www.treasurydirect. gov/NP/debt/current*

80 percent. In 2014, the U.S. national debt was 101.8 percent of the GDP.*

The significance of these two numbers lies within the contrast. The national debt is the amount that needs to be repaid; this can be thought of as the government's credit card balance. The GDP represents the market value of all goods and services produced within a country during a given period. In other words, the GDP represents the gross taxable income available to the government. If debts are increasing at a rate greater than the gross income available for taxation, then the only way to make up the difference is to increase the rate at which the gross income is being taxed.

Since 2011, the national deficit's growth rate has experienced a significant downward trend that is expected to continue throughout 2015. After 2015, however, it is predicted that the deficit will once again begin to increase at an unprecedented rate.** Even more concerning is that the disparity between growth in national debt and growth in GDP is projected to continue, which means the amount of money the federal government owes will far outpace its ability to repay it. As anyone who has struggled with debt can tell you, continually borrowing more money than you make can have potentially disastrous consequences.

The increasing disparity between the debt and GDP rates of growth is not the only disconcerting story: national revenue collection rates offer further cause for concern. Since 1970, the average collection of GDP for revenue was approximately 17.3 percent. In 2012, the collection rate was at 14.4 percent, and rose to above 17 percent in 2014. This increase can be explained by several different tax increases that took place in the intervening

---

* *Federal Reserve Bank of St Louis Economic Research*
** *CBO, An Update to the Budget and Economic Outlook: 2014 - 2024*

years, as well as the effects of recent ROTH conversion limitation removals.

By 2020, it is predicted the revenue rate will rise to be approximately 19.2 percent. When this increase is related to current tax rates, it means that someone currently in the 39.6 percent tax bracket would be pushed into a 44 percent tax bracket. The reality of this projected increase means that additional tax increases are on the horizon, and it would appear that this is going to be a graduated process. Consequently, when the debt ceiling discussions begin again they may be accompanied by a plan to implement additional tax increases over a period of three to five years.

Unfortunately, analysis of the federal government's budget also shows that regardless of revenue collection rates and increased taxes, the deficit will most likely continue to increase, and without additional spending cuts to help bring the budget into balance, tax increases are likely to continue.

THE END OF AN ERA

From a historical point of view, taxes are extremely low. The last time the U.S. national debt was even close to the same percentage level of GDP as it is today was for several years after the end of World War II. The maximum tax rate at that point, and through the years from 1944 through 1963, averaged 90 percent. Compare that to the maximum rate of 39.6 percent today, and it becomes very clear that there is a disparity of extreme proportion.

Taxes during this historical period were at extreme levels for nearly 20 years, throughout and following this level of debt-to-GDP. A significant point to note about the difference at that time versus where we are today is the economic activity. The period of 1944 through 1963 was in the heart of both the Industrial Revolution and the birth of the baby-boom generation. Today, we are mired in extreme volatility with frequent periods of boom and bust accompanied by the beginning of the greatest retirement wave ever experienced within the U.S. economy.

To contrast these two time periods with respect to the recovery period is almost asinine, as the external pressures from globalization and domestic unfunded liabilities did not exist or were irrelevant factors during the prior period.

To add insult to injury, U.S. domestic unfunded liabilities were estimated to be about $84 trillion in 2012 and that number has only increased through the intervening years*. These liabilities exist outside of the annual budgetary debt discussed above and are due to items such as Social Security, Medicare and government pensions. The most concerning part of this stems from the fact that we are on the cusp of the greatest retirement wave in U.S. history as the baby-boom generation begins retiring and drawing from the unfunded Social Security for which they currently have entitlement. Over the long run, expenditures related to healthcare programs such as Medicare and Medicaid are projected to grow faster than the economy overall as the population matures.

To put unfunded liabilities into perspective, consider these as off-balance-sheet obligations similar to those of Enron. Although these are not listed as part of the national debt, they must be paid just the same. The difference between Enron and the U.S. unfunded liabilities is that if the U.S. government cannot come up with the funds to pay all these liabilities through revenue generation then they will print the money necessary to pay the debt.

WHAT DOES THE SOLUTION LOOK LIKE?

Unfortunately, the general public is in a no-win situation for this solution to the problem. Printing money does not bode well for economic growth as this action creates inflationary pressures that

---

* *National Center for Policy Analysis, How Much Does the Federal Government Owe?, June 2012*

devalue the U.S. dollar and make everyone less wealthy. Cutting the entitlements that compose this liability leaves millions of people without benefits they have come to expect. The only other option, and one that the government knows all too well, is increased taxes. In fact, according to a Congressional Budget Office paper issued in 2004*, unfunded liabilities are addressed as follows:

"The term 'unfunded liability' has been used to refer to a gap between the government's projected financial commitment under a particular program and the revenues that are expected to be available to fund that commitment. But no government obligation can be truly considered 'unfunded' because of the U.S. government's sovereign power to tax—which is the ultimate resource to meet its obligations."

A balanced budget is going to be required at some point and with this will come higher taxes. Given our current position and projected budgets, it is likely that tax increases are coming in the near future. However, although raising taxes is a strategy to raise money, it is not a solution to the government's current and pending fiscal problems.

How do you prepare? Why spend so much time reassuring you that taxes will increase? Because you have an opportunity to take action. Now is the time to prepare for what is to come by structuring countermeasures for the good, the bad, and the ugly of each of these legislative nightmares through tax-advantaged retirement planning.

The truth of the matter is that you make more money by saving on taxes than you do by making more money. The simplistic logic of this statement makes sense when you discover it takes a $1.50 in earnings to put that same dollar, saved in taxes, back in

---

* *CBO paper, Measures of the U.S. Government's Fiscal Position Under Current Law, Sept. 2004*

your pocket.* This simple concept becomes extremely valuable to people in retirement and those living on fixed incomes.

As simple as it sounds, it is much more difficult to execute. Most people fail to put together a plan as they near retirement, beginning with a simple cash flow budget. If you have not analyzed your proposed income streams and expenses, you could not possibly have taken the time to position these cash flows and other events into a tax-preferred plan.

Most people will state, "I have a plan" and thus, they do not need any further assistance in this area. The truth in most instances is that many of these people could not show you their plan, and of the few that could, they would not be able to show you how they have executed it. In this regard, they may as well be Richard Nixon saying, "I am not a crook" for as much as they claim, "I have a plan." The truth lies in waiting.

As you approach or begin retirement, you should look at what cash flows you will have. Do you have a pension? How about Social Security? How much additional cash flow are you going to need to draw from your assets to maintain the lifestyle that you desire?

Most people spend their whole lives saving and accumulating wealth but very little time determining a strategy that will distribute this accumulation in ways that will help them to retain it. You need to make sure you have the appropriate diversification of taxable versus non-taxable assets to complement your distribution strategy.

THE BENEFITS OF DIVERSIFICATION

Heading into retirement, you should be situated within a diversified tax landscape. The point to spending your whole life accumulating wealth is not to see how big the number is on paper, but

---

*Assuming a 33 percent effective tax rate

rather to be an exercise in how much you put in your pocket after removing it from the paper.

To truly understand tax diversification, you must understand what types of money exist and how each of these will be treated during accumulation and, most importantly, during distribution. The following is a brief summary:

1. Free money
2. Tax-advantaged money
3. Tax-deferred money
4. Taxable money
    a. Ordinary income
    b. Capital gains and qualified dividends

FREE MONEY

Free money is the best kind of money regardless of the tax treatment, because in the end you have more money than you would have otherwise. Many employers will provide contributions toward employee retirement accounts to offer additional employment benefits and inspire employees to save for their own retirement. With this, employers often will offer a matching contribution in which they will contribute up to a certain percentage of an employee's salary, generally three to five percent, to that employee's retirement account when the employee contributes to their retirement account as well. For example, if an employee earns $50,000 annually and contributes three percent ($1,500) to their retirement account annually, the employer will also contribute three percent ($1,500) to the employee's account. That is $1,500 in free money. Take all that you can get!

TAX-ADVANTAGED MONEY

Tax-advantaged money is the next best thing to free-money. Although you have to earn tax-advantaged money you do not have to give part of it away to Uncle Sam. Tax-advantaged money comes in three basic forms that you can utilize during your lifetime; four if prison inspires your future, but it's not necessary to discuss that option.

One of the most commonly known forms of tax-advantaged money is municipal bonds, which earn and pay interest that could be federally tax-advantaged, state tax-advantaged, or both state and federal tax-advantaged. There are several caveats that should be discussed in regard to the notion of tax-advantaged income from municipal bonds. First, you will notice that tax-advantaged has several flavors from the state and federal perspective. This is because states will generally tax the interest earned on a municipal bond unless the bond is offered from an entity located within that state. This severely limits the availability of completely tax-advantaged municipal bonds and constrains underlying risk and liquidity factors. Second, municipal bond interest gets added back into the equation for determining your modified adjusted gross income (MAGI) for Social Security and could push your income above the thresholds subjecting a portion of your Social Security income to taxation. In effect, if this interest subjects some other income to taxation then this interest is truly being taxed. Last, municipal bond interest may be excluded from the regular federal tax system, but it is included for determining tax under the alternative minimum tax (AMT) system. In its basic form, the AMT system is a separate tax system that applies if the tax computed under AMT exceeds the tax computed under the regular tax system, the difference between these two computations is the alternative minimum tax.

TAX-FREE MONEY: ROTH IRA

Roth accounts are probably the single greatest tax asset that has come from Congress outside of life insurance and are well known but rarely used. Roth IRAs were first established by the Taxpayer Relief Act of 1997 and were named after Senator William Roth, the chief sponsor of the legislation. A Roth account is simply an account in the form of an individual retirement account or an employer-sponsored retirement account that allows for tax-advantaged growth of earnings and, thus, tax-advantaged income.

The main difference between a Roth and a traditional IRA or employer-sponsored plan lies within the timing of the taxation. You're probably very familiar with the typical scenario of putting money away for retirement through an employer plan, whereby your employer deducts money from each paycheck and puts it directly into a retirement account. This money is taken out before taxes are calculated meaning you do not pay tax on those earnings today. A Roth account, on the other hand, takes the money *after* the taxes have been taken out and then puts it into the retirement account, so you do pay tax on the money today. The other significant difference between these two is taxation during distribution in later years. With a traditional retirement account, when you take the money out later it gets added to your ordinary income and is taxed accordingly. Additionally, including this in your income subjects you to the consequences previously mentioned for municipal bonds with Social Security taxation, AMT, as well as higher Medicare premiums. A Roth, on the other hand, has tax-advantaged distributions and does not contribute toward negative impact items such as Social Security taxation, AMT, or Medicare premium increases. It essentially comes back to you without tax and other obligations.

The best way to consider the difference between the two accounts is to look at the life of a farmer. A farmer will buy seed, plant it in the ground, grow the crops, and harvest it later for sale. Typically, the farmer would only pay tax on the crops that have been harvested and sold. But if you were the farmer, would you rather pay tax on $5,000 worth of seed that you plant today or $50,000 worth of harvested crop later? The obvious answer is $5,000 worth of seed today. The truth of the matter is that you are a farmer, except you are planting dollars into your retirement account instead of seeds into the earth.

So why doesn't everyone have a Roth retirement account if things are so simple? There are several reasons, but the single greatest reason has been the constraints on contributions. If you earned over certain thresholds (MAGI over $129,000 single and $191,000 joint for 2014), you were not eligible to make contributions, and, until 2010, if your modified adjusted gross income (MAGI) was over $100,000 (single or joint) then you could not convert a traditional IRA to a Roth. Outside of these contribution limits, most people save for retirement through their employers and most employers are not offering Roth options within their plans. The reason behind this is because Roth accounts are not that well understood and people have been educated to believe that saving on taxes today is the best possible course of action.

TAX-FREE MONEY: LIFE INSURANCE

As previously mentioned, the single greatest tax asset that has come from Congress outside of life insurance is the Roth account. Life insurance is the little known or discussed tax asset that holds some of the greatest value for your financial history both during life and upon death, and it is by far the best tax-advantaged device available. Traditionally, life insurance is viewed as a way to protect your loved ones from financial ruin upon your demise and it should be noted that everyone who cares about someone should have life insurance. By purchasing a life insurance policy, your loved ones will be assured a financial windfall from the life insurance company when you die that will help them with your final expenses and carry on their lives without you comfortably. The best part about the life insurance windfall is the fact that nobody will have to pay tax on the money received. This is the single greatest tax-advantaged device available, but it has one downside, you do not get to use it. Only your heirs will.

The little known and discussed part of life insurance is the cash value build-up within whole life and universal life (permanent) policies. Life insurance is not typically seen as an investment vehicle for building wealth and retirement planning, although it should briefly be discussed why this thought process should be re-evaluated. Permanent life insurance is generally misconceived as something that is very expensive for a wealth accumulation vehicle as there are mortality charges (fees for the death benefit) that detract from the returns that are available and further, those returns do not yield as much as the stock market over the long run. This is why many times you will hear the phrase "buy term and invest the rest," where "term" refers to term insurance.

It's important to review the two terms just used in regard to life insurance: term and permanent. Term insurance is what most people are familiar with. You purchase a certain death benefit that will go to your heirs upon your death and this policy will be in effect for a certain number of years, typically 10 to 20 years. The 10 to 20 years is the term of the policy and once you have reached that end you no longer have insurance unless you purchase another policy at that point.

On the other hand, permanent insurance has no term involved, it is permanent as long as the premiums continue to be paid. Permanent insurance generally has higher premiums than term insurance for the same amount of death benefit coverage and it is this difference that is referred to when people say "invest the rest."

Simply speaking, there are significant differences between these two policies that do not get taken into consideration when providing a comparative analysis in the numbers. One item that gets lost in the fray when comparing term and permanent insurance is that term usually expires before death, in fact insurance studies show less than 1 percent of all term policies pay out death benefit claims. The issue arises when the term expires and the desire to have more insurance is still present. A term policy with the same benefit will be much more expensive than the original policy and, many times, life events occur, such as cancer or heart conditions, which makes it impossible to acquire another policy and leaves your loved ones unprotected and tax-advantaged legacy planning out of the equation.

Another aspect and probably the most important piece in consideration of the future of taxation is the fact that permanent insurance has a cash accumulation value. Two aspects stand out with the cash accumulation value. First, as the cash accumulation value increases, the death benefit will also increase whereas term insurance is level. Second, this cash accumulation offers value to you during your lifetime rather than just your heirs upon death. The cash accumulation value can be used for tax-advantaged income during your lifetime through policy loans. Most importantly, this tax-advantaged income is available during retirement for distribution planning, all while offering the same typical financial protection to your heirs.

TAX-DEFERRED MONEY

Tax-deferred money is the type of money from which most people are familiar, but the idea was also briefly reviewed above. Tax-deferred money is typically your traditional IRA, employer sponsored retirement plan, or a non-qualified annuity. Essentially, money is put into an investment vehicle that will accumulate in value over time and you do not pay taxes on the earnings that grow in these accounts until it is distributed. Taxes must be paid once the money is distributed and, in addition to the taxes, the same negative consequences exist toward additional taxation and expense in other areas as previously discussed.

TAXABLE MONEY

Taxable money is everything else and is taxable both today and later, whenever it is received.

Of these four types of money, they really come down to two distinct classifications: taxable and tax-advantaged.

The greatest difference when comparing taxable and tax-advantaged income is a function of how much money you will keep after tax. For help in determining what the differences should be, excluding outside factors such as Social Security taxation and AMT, a tax equivalent yield should be used.

TAX-FREE IN THE REAL WORLD

To put the tax equivalent yield into perspective, consider the following example:

> » Bob and Mary are currently retired and in the 25 percent tax bracket living on Social Security and interest from investments. They have a substantial portion of their investments in municipal bonds yielding 6.0 percent, which in today's market is quite comforting. The tax equivalent yield they would need to earn from a taxable investment would be 8.0 percent, a 2.0 percent gap which seems almost impossible given current market volatility. However, something that has never been put into perspective is that the interest from their municipal bonds is subject to taxation on their Social Security benefits* (at 21.25 percent). With this, the yield on their municipal bonds would be 4.725 percent**, and the taxable equivalent yield falls to 6.3 percent leaving a gap of only 1.575 percent.

In the end, most people spend their lives accumulating wealth through the best, if not only vehicle they know, a tax-deferred account. This account is most likely a 401(k) or 403(b) plan offered

---

* Assuming each dollar of interest subjects a dollar of Social Security income to taxation at 85 percent

** 6.0 percent – (6.0 percent -21.25 percent) = 4.725 percent

through your employer and may be supplemented with an IRA that was established at one point or another. As the years go by, people blindly throw money into these accounts in an effort to save for a retirement that they someday hope to reach.

The truth is most people have an age selected for when they would like to retire but spend their lives wondering if they will ever be able to actually quit working. To answer this question, you must understand how much money you will have available to contribute toward your needs. In other words, you need to know what your after-tax income will be during this period.

All else being equal, it would not matter if you put your money into a taxable, tax-deferred, or tax-advantaged account as long as income tax rates never change and outside factors are never an event. The net amount you receive in the end will be the same. Unfortunately, this will never be the case. We already know that taxes will increase in the future, meaning we will likely see higher taxes in retirement than during our peak earning years.

Regardless, saving for retirement in any form is a good thing since it appears from all practical perspectives that future government benefits will be cut and taxes will increase. You have the ability to plan today for efficient tax diversification and maximization of your after-tax dollars during your distribution years.

CHAPTER 10 RECAP //

- The future of U.S. taxation is uncertain. You know what the tax rate and landscape is today, but you won't tomorrow. The only thing you can really count on is the trend of increasing taxation.
- Most people are familiar with tax-deferred methods of retirement savings such as traditional IRAs. By taking action now, you can prepare for the rise in taxes by restructuring your assets to include the benefits of tax-advantaged money.
- Tax-advantaged money is money you earn without having to pay taxes on. One of the most common forms includes municipal bonds, but be aware these come with many state and federal caveats and complexities.
- Roth IRAs and life insurance policies are two forms of tax-advantaged money that can take advantage of today's lower tax rate when preparing for tomorrow's retirement.

11

SCORE NOW AND WIN LATER:
HOW TO TIME ROTH CONVERSIONS

Louis Brandeis provides one of the best examples illustrating how proactive tax planning works. Brandeis was Associate Justice on the Supreme Court of the United States from 1916 to 1939. Born in Louisville, Kentucky, Brandeis was an intelligent man with a touch of country charm. He described tax planning this way:

"I live in Alexandria, Virginia. Near the Court Chambers, there is a toll bridge across the Potomac. When in a rush, I pay the dollar toll and get home early. However, I usually drive outside the downtown section of the city and cross the Potomac on a free bridge.

The bridge was placed outside the downtown Washington, D.C. area to serve a useful social service—getting drivers to drive the extra mile and help alleviate congestion during the rush hour.

If I went over the toll bridge and through the barrier without paying a toll, I would be committing tax evasion.

If I drive the extra mile and drive outside the city of Washington to the free bridge, I am using a legitimate, logical and suitable method of tax avoidance, and I am performing a useful social service by doing so.

*The tragedy is that **few people know that the free bridge exists.***"

Like Brandeis, most American taxpayers have options when it comes to "crossing the Potomac," so to speak. It's a financial planner's job to tell you what options are available. You can wait until March to file your taxes, at which time you might pay someone to report and pay the government a larger portion of your income. However, you could instead file before the end of the year, work with your financial professional and incorporate a tax plan as part of your overall financial planning strategy. Filing later is like crossing the toll bridge. Tax planning is like crossing the free bridge.

Which would you rather do?

The answer to this question is easy. Most people want to save money and pay less in taxes. What makes this situation really difficult in real life, however, is that the signs along the side of the road that direct us to the free bridge are not that clear. To normal Americans, and to plenty of people who have studied it, the U.S. tax code is easy to get lost in. There are all kinds of rules, exceptions to rules, caveats and conditions that are difficult to understand, or even to know about. What you really need to know is your options and the bottom line impacts of those options.

ROTH IRA CONVERSIONS

The attractive qualities of Roth IRAs may have prompted you to explore the possibility of moving some of your assets into a Roth account. You might think of this as scoring now and winning later, because taking money out of your qualified account will result in a sum of money that you pay taxes on now for the reward of a tax-free retirement down the road. Another important difference between the accounts is how they treat Required Minimum Distributions (RMDs). When you turn 70 ½ years old, you are required to take a minimum amount of money out of a traditional IRA. This amount is your RMD. It is treated as taxable income. Roth IRAs, however, do not have RMDs, and their distributions are not taxable. Quite a deal, right?

While having a Roth IRA as part of your portfolio is a good idea, converting assets to a Roth IRA can pose some challenges, depending on what kinds of assets you want to transfer.

One common option is the conversion of a traditional IRA to a Roth IRA. You may have heard about converting your IRA to a Roth IRA, but you might not know the full net result on your income. The main difference between the two accounts is that the growth of investments within a traditional IRA is not taxed until income is withdrawn from the account, whereas taxes are charged on contribution amounts to a Roth IRA, not withdrawals. The problem, however, is that when assets are removed from a traditional IRA, even if the assets are being transferred to a Roth IRA account, taxes apply.

There are a lot of reasons to look at Roth conversions. People have a lot of money in IRAs, up to multiple millions of dollars. Even with $500,000, when they turn 70 ½ years old, their RMD is going to be approximately $18,000, and they have to take that out whether they want to or not. It's a tax issue. Essentially, if you will be subject to high RMDs, it could have impacts on how much of your Social Security is taxable, and on your tax bracket.

By paying taxes now instead of later on assets in a Roth IRA, you can realize tax-advantaged growth. You pay once and you're done paying. Your heirs are done paying. It's a powerful tool. Here's a simple example to show you how powerful it can be: *Imagine that you pay to convert a traditional IRA to a Roth. You have decided that you want to put the money in a vehicle that gives you a tax-advantaged income option down the road. If you pay a 25 percent tax on that conversion and the Roth IRA then doubles in value over the next 10 years, you could look at your situation as only having paid 12.5 percent tax.*

The prospect of tax-advantaged income is a tempting one. While you have to pay a conversion tax to transfer your assets, you also have turned taxable income into tax free retirement money that you can let grow as long as you want without being required to withdraw it.

There are options, however, that address this problem. Much like the Brandeis story, there may be a "free bridge" option for many investors.

Your financial professional will likely tell you that it is not a matter of whether or not you should perform a Roth IRA conversion, it is a matter of how much you should convert and when.

Here are some of the things to consider before converting to a Roth IRA:

- If you make a conversion before you retire, you may end up paying higher taxes on the conversion because it is likely that you are in some of your highest earning years, placing you in the highest tax bracket of your life. It is possible that a better strategy would be to wait until after you retire, a time when you may have less taxable income, which would place you in a lower tax bracket.
- Many people opt to reduce their work hours from fulltime to part-time in the years before they retire. If you have

pursued this option, your income will likely be lower, in turn lowering your tax rate.

- The first years that you draw Social Security benefits can also be years of lower reported income, making it another good time frame in which to convert to a Roth IRA.

One key strategy to handling a Roth IRA conversion is to *always be able to pay the cost of the tax conversion with outside money*. Structuring your tax year to include something like a significant deduction can help you offset the conversion tax. This way you aren't forced to take the money you need for taxes from the value of the IRA. The reason taxes apply to this maneuver is because when you withdraw money from a traditional IRA, it is treated as taxable income by the IRS. Your financial professional, with the help of the CPAs at their firm, may be able to provide you with options like after-tax money, itemized deductions or other situations that can pose effective tax avoidance options.

Some examples of avoiding Roth IRA conversions taxes include:

- *Using medical expenses that are above 10 percent of your Adjusted Gross Income.* If you have health care costs that you can list as itemized deductions, you can convert an amount of income from a traditional IRA to a Roth IRA that is offset by the deductible amount. Essentially, deductible medical expenses negate the taxes resulting from recording the conversion.
- *Individuals, usually small business owners, who are dealing with a Net Operating Loss (NOL).* If you have NOLs, but aren't able to utilize all of them on your tax return, you can carry them forward to offset the taxable income from the taxes on income you convert to a Roth IRA.
- *Charitable giving.* If you are charitably inclined, you can use the amount of your donations to reduce the amount

of taxable income you have during that year. By matching the amount you convert to a Roth IRA to the amount your taxable income was reduced by charitable giving, you can essentially avoid taxation on the conversion. You may decide to double your donations to a charity in one year, giving them two years' worth of donations in order to offset the Roth IRA conversion tax on this year's tax return.

- *Investments that are subject to depletion.* Certain investments can kick off depletion expenses. If you make an investment and are subject to depletion expenses, they can be deducted and used to offset a Roth IRA conversion tax.

Not all of the above scenarios work for everyone, and there are many other options for offsetting conversion taxes. The point is that you have options, and your financial professional and tax professional can help you understand those options.

If you have a traditional IRA, Roth conversions are something you should look at. As you approach retirement you should consider your options and make choices that keep more of your money in your pocket, not the government's.

ADDITIONAL TAX BENEFITS OF ROTH IRAS

Not only do Roth IRAs provide you with tax-advantaged growth, they also give you a tax diversified landscape that allows you to maximize your distributions. Chances are that no matter the circumstances, you will have taxed income and other assets subject to taxation. *But if you have a Roth IRA, you have the unique ability to manage your Adjusted Gross Income (AGI), because you have a tax-advantaged income option!*

Converting to a Roth IRA can also help you preserve and build your legacy. Because Roth IRAs are exempt from RMDs, after you make a conversion from a traditional IRA, your Roth account can grow tax-advantaged for another 15, 20 or 25 years and it can be used as tax-advantaged income by your heirs. It is important to note, however, that non-spousal beneficiaries do have to take RMDs from a Roth IRA, or choose to stretch it and draw tax-advantaged income out of it over their lifetime.

TO CONVERT OR NOT TO CONVERT?

Conversions aren't only for retirees. You can convert at any time. Your choice should be based on your individual circumstances and tax situation. Sticking with a traditional IRA or converting to a Roth, again, depends on your individual circumstances, including your income, your tax bracket and the amount of deductions you have each year.

Is it better to have a Roth IRA or traditional IRA? It depends on your individual circumstance. Some people don't mind having taxable income from an IRA. Their income might not be very high and their RMD might not bump their tax bracket up, so it's not as big a deal. A similar situation might involve income from Social Security. Social Security benefits are taxed based on other income you are drawing. If you are in a position where none or very little of your Social Security benefit is subject to taxes, paying income tax on your RMD may be very easy.

> » *There are also situations where leveraging taxable income from a traditional IRA can work to your advantage come tax time. For example, David and Emily dream of buying a boat when they retire. It is something they have looked forward to their entire marriage. In addition to the savings and investments that they created to supply them with income during retirement, which includes a traditional IRA, they have also saved money for the sole purpose of purchasing a boat once they stop working.*

When the time comes and they finally buy the boat of their dreams, they pay an additional $15,000 in sales taxes that year because of the large purchase. Because they are retired and earning less money, the deductions they used to be able to realize from their income taxes are no longer there. The high amount of sales taxes they paid on the boat puts them in a position where they could benefit from taking taxable income from a traditional IRA.

When David and Emily's financial professional learns about their purchase, he immediately contacts a CPA at his firm to run the numbers. They determine that by taking a $15,000 distribution from their IRA, they could fulfill their income needs to offset the $15,000 sales tax deduction that they were claiming due to the purchase of their boat. In the end, they pay zero taxes on their income distribution from their IRA.

The moral of the story? **Having a tax-diversified landscape gives you options.** Having capital assets that can be liquidated, tax-advantaged income options and sources that can create capital gains or capital losses will put you in a position to play your cards right no matter what you want to accomplish with your taxes. The ace up your sleeve is your financial professional and the CPAs they work with. Do yourself a favor and *plan* your taxes instead of *reporting* them!

CHAPTER 11 RECAP //

- Given that the future of U.S. taxation is certain to bring an increase, a Roth Conversion allows you to pay your taxes ahead of time while in a lower tax bracket.
- Look for the "free bridge" option in your tax strategy.
- Converting from a traditional to a Roth IRA can provide you with tax-advantaged retirement income.
- Converting to a Roth IRA can also help you preserve and build your legacy.

12
THE SECRET TO LONG-TERM CARE PLANNING

The U.S. Department of Health and Human Services estimates that 70 percent of Americans who reach the age of 65 will need some kind of long-term care for at least three years during their lifetime. *

There is a lot of confusion about the meaning of the word, long-term care. Most people hear this term and a nursing home pops right into their minds. While a long-term care situation could certainly involve a nursing home, the reality nowadays is that long-term care looks quite a bit different. Assisted living facilities,

---

* *http://longtermcare.gov/the-basics/who-needs-care/*

adult day care and home health care all fall under the long-term care umbrella, and most people actually receive services from the comfort of their own homes.* There are also a lot more choices and options when it comes to paying for these services than most people realize.

The cost of long-term care services is one of the most formidable opponents to the security of your retirement savings. In life as in sports, the more you know about your opponent, the better your chances for victory. This chapter is designed to give you the facts about what long-term care is, who needs it and how you can prepare. The solutions offered here aren't your typical options, but rather represent a more comprehensive overview to help you better prepare for the challenges that come with the gift of increased longevity.

KNOW YOUR OPPONENT

Most people make the mistake of thinking they have to be sick in order to need long-term care, but the term really refers to a range of services, the most common of which include basic daily living tasks. Menial custodial chores such as taking out the garbage, shopping for food, and other necessities can get harder to do as we age and our bodies get tired. This is especially true for people who are living alone. Aging is a process and long-term care situations can also develop gradually over the course of several years. So what kinds of ailments qualify you for long-term care?

Custodial services are one kind of long-term care that might not have anything to do with a diagnosed medical condition. This is often the case for elderly widows or single persons who might need a little extra help performing every-day tasks. These tasks, known in the industry as Instrumental Activities of Daily Living

---

* *http://longtermcare.gov/the-basics/where-can-you-receive-care/*

(or IADLs), are necessary for independent living and they include the following:

- Housework
- Managing money
- Taking medication
- Preparing and cleaning up after meals
- Shopping for groceries or clothes
- Using the telephone or other communication devices
- Caring for pets
- Responding to emergency alerts such as fire alarms*

For families who live near one another, long-term care planning might involve sons and daughters helping mothers and fathers with these IADLs, which is why having a conversation with your family members about your concerns is particularly important. For working families who need help, adult day care facilities offer activities and companionship. A working son or daughter, or even a retired spouse, can leave their loved one at a facility during the day for a certain number of hours, then pick them up on the way home. This can be a great way for family caregivers to get a little extra support. The group atmosphere also makes this care a little more affordable. The Genworth Cost of Care Survey for 2014 lists the median rate at $52 daily for adult day care centers in the state of Ohio.**

Most people who use long-term care service do so because they need help with basic personal tasks such as bathing, getting dressed or help getting up from a chair.*** The Department of Human Services has identified the six activities of daily living (known

---

* http://longtermcare.gov/the-basics/what-is-long-term-care/

** https://www.genworth.com/dam/Americas/US/PDFs/Consumer/corporate/Ohio-040114.pdf

*** http://longtermcare.gov/the-basics/what-is-long-term-care/

as ADLs) that are necessary for daily life. These activities include the following tasks:

- Bathing
- Dressing
- Using the toilet
- Transferring (to or from bed or chair)
- Caring for incontinence
- Eating*

While you might not need a medical degree to perform these tasks, they can be physically difficult to perform, which is why many families find it necessary to hire professional help. Basic homemaker services start at $13 an hour for non-skilled services in the state of Ohio, and go all the way up to $31 an hour for more skilled nursing services by a home health aide.**

When you or a loved one starts to have difficulty with two or more of these ADLs, you are able to qualify for long-term care benefits. For cases where there is a medical condition or memory issues, a facility stay may be needed. These costs can vary greatly depending on the facility and the type of care needed, but the average cost for a semi-private room in a nursing home for the state of Ohio is $67,890 - $74,460 a year.***

CHOOSE YOUR STRATEGY

The average duration for long-term care services is three years, but 20 percent of people who need long-term care will require services for 5 or more years. If you are retiring today at the age of 65 and will require care at the age of 90, 25 years will pass before you

---

* http://longtermcare.gov/the-basics/what-is-long-term-care/

** https://www.genworth.com/dam/Americas/US/PDFs/Consumer/corporate/Ohio-040114.pdf

*** http://longtermcare.gov/costs-how-to-pay/costs-of-care-in-your-state/

need the assistance. How expensive will long-term care be in 25 years? It's hard to know, and even harder to think about, which is why the secret to long-term care planning is to think about it in terms of simple income streams. When protecting your assets and your loved ones, don't think about it as planning to get sick, *think of it as planning for additional streams of income that you can turn on later should either you or your spouse ever need care.*

When you plan for more income, the burden of an additional monthly expense is written into the plan. With asset-based options offered by insurance companies today, should you never need to turn the income stream on, the money will go to your beneficiaries. Retirees today have many options when it comes to creating these additional income streams, and there are new rules and programs that also give tax incentives to those who do plan. While the following list is by no means exhaustive, it covers the basics. We will start with the option most people are familiar with:

Option #1: Traditional Long-term Care Insurance
Traditional Long-term Care Insurance offers the most comprehensive kind of care. These policies saw their glory days in the 1980s. Many of them are no longer available today, and most retirees find them expensive and difficult to qualify for. The story below illustrates how this older strategy might turn out to be a losing proposition for the average husband and wife team:

> » *When Gary and Marie were in their late 50s, they purchased a traditional long-term care insurance policy because their grown children all lived in different states. They didn't want their children to have to worry about taking care of them, so they paid in the $5,000 annual premium faithfully for 30 years. Gary and Marie also took care of themselves, ate well and exercised. They also had good genes. They lived to the*

ages of 87 and 89 respectively without ever needing any form of long-term care. Gary and Marie beat the odds, but they didn't get to spend any of the $150,000 they paid into their policy. This money didn't go to them and it didn't go to their kids; instead, it all went to the insurance company.

While using an insurance company to help leverage your dollars is a great way to transfer risk, today's retirees have more options than these traditional use-it-or-lose-it policies. The federal government has recognized the strain on Medicaid that comes with being the primary provider of long-term care. To encourage U.S. citizens to be more proactive with their long-term care planning, they have offered new tax incentives. The Pension Protection Act was passed in 2006 and went into effect on January 1 of 2010. Section 844 of the act allows for income from qualified annuity contracts used to pay for long-term care to be withdrawn tax-free.* This is great news, because taking out more income to pay for long-term care can have many negative percussions from a tax standpoint.

Insurance companies have also realized that traditional long-term care insurance is not a popular choice: according to the National Care Planning Council, less than 10 percent of individuals over the age of 65 own long-term care insurance.** By using our secret formula—looking for ways to create additional streams of income that can be turned on at the time of need—you can use these tax incentives and newer policies to your advantage.

Option #2: The Hybrid Option: Single Premium Life
Like an electric car that can get 50 to 80 miles per gallon, Single Premium Life Insurance offers better mileage for your dollar with different ways to power the engine, so to speak. You also might

---

* *http://www.irs.gov/irb/2011-36_IRB/ar08.html*
** *https://www.longtermcarelink.net/eldercare/long_term_care_insurance.htm*

think of it as a hybrid option because it gives you the best of both worlds: leveraged long-term care benefits built right into the policy, and a death benefit for your beneficiaries should you never need long-term care. The following story illustrates how a hybrid solution can help you create an additional stream of income when you need it most:

> » *Art and Mary have $85,000 sitting in a bank CD that they have earmarked as their long-term care fund. Because Art is eight years older than Mary and not in the best of health, he wants her to have a way to pay for help should he ever get sick. As part of their comprehensive income plan, Art and Mary use their $85,000 to purchase a single premium life insurance policy with an accelerated benefit guaranteed to provide them with $250,000 in long-term care benefits.*
>
> *Five years later, Art's physical condition worsens and he is unable to get out of bed or into a bath without assistance. At the age of 73, Mary is unable to lift her husband by herself. The couple finds that they need assistance. Because Art is unable to perform two of the six activities of daily living, Mary is able to trigger the long-term care benefit on their life insurance policy without any worry or stress. According to the terms of their particular contract, they will receive an additional $2,000 a month in income. With this additional income stream, Mary is able to hire an at-home health care aid to come out to the house. Their policy gave them an additional $24,000 of income a year, and best of all, this money doesn't count against them as taxable income. They weren't thrown into a higher tax bracket. Art got the care he needed, and Mary got the help she needed because they were able to turn on an additional income stream at the time when they needed it most.*

There are two ways you can fund a single premium life insurance policy. If you don't have a lump sum like Art and Mary did, you can choose what's called a 10-Pay and fund the policy over the course of a 10-year period of time. Each funding option has different pros and cons, but in general, these hybrid policies are extremely liquid investments. You can terminate the policy at any time, and you have access to 90 percent of the cash value of the policy. Perhaps the most attractive feature is that should you never have a qualifying event, your beneficiary receives the full value of the death benefit, so the money paid into the policy is never lost.

Option #3: The Annuity Option
We talked earlier how a rider on a fixed indexed annuity can provide you with a guaranteed stream of lifetime income. This is the most common rider with fixed indexed annuities, but it's not the only rider. There are other riders available that address the concerns of long-term care. Some of these riders cost a fee while others do not. These riders give annuitants a way to access the money they have put into the contract without penalties or surrender charges. These riders can also provide a long-term care benefit payout that is much higher than the actual value of the annuity. Furthermore, thanks to the Pension Protection Act, when the income stream is turned on to pay for long-term care, this money is received tax-free, if it is a non-qualified annuity.

> » *Mark and Kristi have $140,000 in an annuity with a long-term care benefit associated with the premium. They think of it as their long-term care annuity because it will pay out up to $500,000 in additional income should either Mark or Kristi ever need to fund long-term care. If neither of them needs the care, then their children will receive the actual value of the annuity.*

As with the pervious option, the inability to perform two out of the six ADLs triggers the benefit, which can also include funding basic custodial services such as cleaning and taking out the garbage, or more involved intrinsic nursing services. The benefits and terms of the policy vary according to your age and health and the underwriters of the insurance company. What's nice about these life insurance and annuity options, however, is that when the insurance company pays you the money, you can choose what type of care to spend the money on.

Unlike the traditional use-it-or-lose-it plans of the past, these are USE IT plans. Either you will use the money now, while you are alive, or your beneficiaries will.

Option #4: Aid And Attendance
There is another solution available to veterans and their surviving spouses who require the regular attendance of another person to assist in the six activities of daily living. There are a number of criteria that may affect your eligibility, and filing time is also important. In general, this benefit is available to qualified individuals who reside in assisted living communities, personal care homes, skilled nursing facilities and those receiving personal in-home care. Unlike the aforementioned options, you don't have to pay anything in order to receive this benefit. Your service in the military qualifies you and is the first eligibility requirement. Once qualified, the Aid and Attendance benefit will payout an additional stream of income every month to help pay for long-term care services.

If you think you might qualify for this benefit, or you know somebody who you believe may be eligible, bring this to the attention of your financial professional. Not all advisors have the qualifications needed to help retirees apply for this option. To submit your application, you want to work with someone who specializes in this area, such as an elder law attorney who is VA accredited.

GET YOUR FAMILY IN ON THE PLAY

Perhaps the most important aspect of long-term care planning is communicating your wishes. Nothing beats having well worded legal estate planning documents along with a good, frank discussion with your family members and children. Discussing the issue, as unpleasant as it might seem, is a critical component. Best of all, it's free. If the unexpected ever happens, your family members need to know how to approach it and how they can help. Things to discuss might include:

- What do you want?
- What do you expect of your kids?
- What are your kids willing and able to do?

Health-care directives and other legal paperwork can be completed at no cost or for a nominal fee. Ask your financial professional about these no and low-cost options as part of your overall comprehensive plan.

In closing, you might not be able to craft the perfect solution for every possible scenario, but just having your paperwork in order and having a conversation with your loved ones is better than avoiding the issue. Do the best that you can afford. Even if it's not the perfect solution, having at least one play is better than having no play at all.

CHAPTER 12 RECAP //

- According to the U.S. Department of Health and Human Services, 70 percent of people turning 65 years old today will require some kind of long-term care during their life.

- Long-term care refers to a wide range of services, from help with grocery shopping to intrinsic medical care in an assisted living facility or nursing home. Most people use long-term care not because they are sick, but because they need help with basic personal tasks such as bathing or getting up from a chair or bed.

- When you think of your long-term care planning in terms of an income strategy, you don't have to worry about trying to qualify or afford the use-it-or-lose-it traditional long-term care policies.

- Traditional long-term care insurance can be expensive and if it is not used, the money paid into the policy is lost. With asset-based life insurance and annuity solutions, the money is not lost should the policyholder never need care. Instead, the money is passed along to the named beneficiaries.

- Perhaps the most impactful thing you can do as part of your plan is free: have a conversation with your family members. Nothing beats having good legal documents in place and communicating your wishes to those you love.

.

13
YOUR LEGACY BEYOND DOLLARS AND CENTS

If you're like most people, planning your estate isn't on the top of your list of things to do. Planning your income needs for retirement, managing your assets and just living your life without worrying about how your estate will be handled when you are gone make legacy planning less than attractive for a Saturday afternoon task. The fact of the matter, however, is that if you don't plan your legacy, someone else will. That someone else is usually a combination of the IRS and other government entities: lawyers, executors, courts, and accountants. Who do you think has the best interests of your beneficiaries in mind?

WHAT'S YOUR DEFINITION OF LEGACY?

Today, there is more consideration given to planning a legacy than just maximizing your estate. When most people think about an estate, it may seem like something only the very wealthy have: a stately manor or an enormous business. But a legacy is something else entirely. A legacy is more than the sum total of the financial assets you have accumulated. It is the lasting impression you make on those you leave behind. The dollar and cents are just a small part of a legacy.

A legacy encompasses the stories that others tell about you, shared experiences and values. An estate may pay for college tuition, but a legacy may inform your grandchildren about the importance of higher education and self-reliance.

A legacy may also contain family heirlooms or items of emotional significance. It may be a piece of art your great-grandmother painted, family photos, or a childhood keepsake.

When you go about planning your legacy, certainly explore strategies that can maximize the financial benefit to the ones you care about. But also take the time to ensure that you have organized the whole of your legacy, and let that be a part of the last gift you leave.

Many people avoid planning their legacy until they feel they must. Something may change in your life, like the birth of a grandchild, the diagnosis of a serious health problem, or the death of a close friend or loved one. Waiting for tragedy to strike in order to get your affairs in order is not the best course of action. The emotional stress of that kind of situation can make it hard to make patient, thoughtful decisions. Taking the time to create a premeditated and thoughtful legacy plan will assure that your assets will be transferred where and when you want them when the time comes.

THE SEVENTH INNING STRETCH: BENEFITS OF PLANNING YOUR LEGACY

The distribution of your assets, whether in the form of property, stocks, Individual Retirement Accounts, 401(k)s or liquid assets, can be a complicated undertaking if you haven't left clear instructions about how you want them handled. Not having a plan will cost more money and take more time, leaving your loved ones to wait (sometimes for years) and receive less of your legacy than if you had a clear plan.

Planning your legacy will help your assets be transferred with little delay and little confusion. Instead of leaving decisions about how to distribute your estate to your family, attorneys or financial professionals, preserve your legacy and your wishes by drafting a clear plan at an early age.

And while you know all that, it can still be hard to sit down and do it. It reminds you that life is short, and the relatively complicated nature of sorting through your assets can feel like a daunting task. But one thing is for sure: *it is impossible for your assets to be transferred or distributed the way you want at the end of your life if you don't have a plan.*

Ask yourself:
- Are my assets up to date?
- Have my primary and contingent beneficiaries been clearly designated?
- Does my plan allow for restriction of a beneficiary?
- Does my legacy plan address minor children that I want to provide with income?
- Does my legacy plan allow for multi-generational payout?

Answers to these questions are critical if you want the final say in how your assets are distributed. In order to achieve your legacy goals, you need a plan.

MAKING A GAME PLAN

Eventually, when your income need is filled and you have sufficient standby money to meet your need for emergencies, travel or other extra expenses you are planning for, whatever isn't used during your lifetime becomes your financial legacy. The money that you do not use during your lifetime will either go to loved ones, unloved ones, charity, or the IRS. The question is, who would you rather disinherit?

By having a legacy plan that clearly outlines your assets, your beneficiaries and your distribution goals, you can make sure that your money and property is ending up in the hands of the people you determine beforehand. Is it really that big of a deal? It absolutely is. Think about it. Without a clear plan, it is impossible for anyone to know if your beneficiary designations are current and reflect your wishes because you haven't clearly expressed who your beneficiaries are. You may have an idea of who you want your assets to go to, but without a plan, it is anyone's guess. It is also impossible to know if the titling of your assets is accurate unless you have gone through and determined whose name is on the titles. More importantly, *if you have not clearly and effectively communicated your desires regarding the planned distribution of your legacy, you and your family may end up losing a large part of it.*

As you can see, managing a legacy is more complicated than having an attorney read your will, divide your estate and write checks to your heirs. The additional issue of taxes, Family Maximum Benefit calculations and a host of other decisions rear their heads. Educating yourself about the best options for positioning your legacy assets is a challenging undertaking. Working with a financial professional who is versed in determining the most efficient and effective ways of preserving and distributing your legacy can save you time, money and strife.

So, how do you begin?

Making a Legacy Plan Starts with a Simple List. The first, and one of the largest, steps to setting up an estate plan with a financial professional that reflects your desires is creating a detailed inventory of your assets and debts (if you have any). You need to know what assets you have, who the beneficiaries are, how much they are worth and how they are titled. You can start by identifying and listing your assets. This is a good starting point for working with a financial professional who can then help you determine the detailed information about your assets that will dictate how they are distributed upon your death.

If you are particularly concerned about leaving your kids and grandkids a lifetime of income with minimal taxes, you will want to discuss a Stretch IRA option with your financial professional.

STRETCH IRAS: GETTING THE MOST OUT OF YOUR MONEY

In 1986, the U.S. Congress passed a law that allows for multi-generational distributions of IRA assets. This type of distribution is called a Stretch IRA because it stretches the distribution of the account out over a longer period of time to several beneficiaries. It also allows the account to continue accumulating value throughout your relatives' lifetimes. You can use a Stretch IRA as an income tool that distributes throughout your lifetime, your children's lifetimes and your grandchildren's lifetimes.

Stretch IRAs are an attractive option for those more concerned with creating income for their loved ones than leaving them with a lump sum that may be subject to a high tax rate. With traditional IRA distributions, non-spousal beneficiaries must generally take distributions from their inherited IRAs, whether transferred or not, within five years after the death of the IRA owner. An exception to this rule applies if the beneficiary elects to take distributions over his or her lifetime, which is referred to as stretching the IRA.

Let's begin by looking at the potential of stretching an IRA throughout multiple generations.

As the illustrations with the Cleaver family show, stretching an IRA over multiple generations can have a large impact on the total amount of income that it is able to provide. In the top illustration,

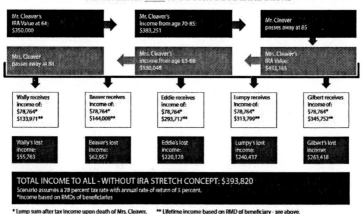

Mr. Cleaver's IRA is stretched so it provides his children with multiple distributions throughout their lifetimes. By the time the account is empty, Mr. Cleaver's $350,000 IRA has been turned into a legacy of more than $1.2 million for the entire Cleaver family. But look at what happens when the IRA is not stretched: after Mr. and Mrs. Cleaver pass away, the IRA is divided between the five children and distributed to each as a single lump sum. In that scenario, the IRA only provides the Cleaver family with a total income of $393,820. For the Cleavers, not choosing to stretch the IRA would cost them nearly $800,000 in lost income.

Unfortunately, many things may also play a role in failing to stretch IRA distributions. It can be tempting for a beneficiary to take a lump sum of money despite the tax consequences. Fortunately, if you want to solidify your plan for distribution, there are options that will allow you to open up an IRA and incorporate "spendthrift" clauses for your beneficiaries. This will ensure your legacy is stretched appropriately and to your specifications. Only certain insurance companies allow this option, and you will not find this benefit with any brokerage accounts. You need to work with a financial professional who has the appropriate relationship with an insurance company that provides this option.

CHAPTER 13 RECAP //

- The IRS can be one of your biggest beneficiaries if you don't take the time to do proper estate planning. The money that you do not use during your lifetime will either go to loved ones, a charity, or the IRS. Ask yourself, who would you rather disinherit?
- With a traditional IRA, your beneficiaries may inherit your tax burden depending on where that money came from.
- Failing to maximize your legacy can cost your beneficiaries thousands of dollars. With the counsel of a financial professional, it's possible to structure your assets in ways that maximize distributions to your beneficiaries, but for best results, the plan must be made before you pass away.
- Stretch IRAs give beneficiaries the option of taking smaller distributions over the course of their lifetime, which allows them to take advantage of interest compounded over several years.
- Legacy planning begins with a simple list.

14

PREPARING FOR THE END OF THE GAME

Matthew organized his assets long ago. He started planning his retirement early and made investment decisions that would meet his needs. With a combination of IRA to Roth IRA conversions, a series of income annuities and a well-planned money management strategy overseen by his financial professional, he easily filled his income gap and was able to focus on ways to accumulate his wealth throughout his retirement. He reorganized his Know So and Hope So Money as he got older. When Matthew retired, he had an income plan created that allowed him to maximize his Social Security benefit. He even had enough to accumulate wealth during his retirement. At this point, Matthew turned his attention to planning his legacy. He wanted to know how he could maximize the amount of his legacy he will pass on to his heirs.

Matthew met with an attorney to draw up a will, but he quickly learned that while having a will was a good plan, it wasn't the most efficient way to distribute his legacy. In fact, relying solely on a will created several roadblocks.

The two main problems that arose for Matthew were *Probate* and *Unintentional Disinheritance:*

Problem #1: Probate

Probate. Just speaking the word out loud can cause shivers to run down your spine. Probate's ugly reputation is well deserved. It can be a costly, time consuming process that diminishes your estate and can delay the distribution of your estate to your loved ones. Nasty stuff, by any measure. Unless you have made a clear legacy plan and discussed options for avoiding probate, it is highly likely that you have many assets that might pass through probate needlessly. ***If your will and beneficiary designations aren't correctly structured, some of these assets will go through the probate process, which can turn dollars into cents.***

If you have a will, probate is usually just a formality. There is little risk that your will won't be executed per your instructions. The problem arises when the costs and lengthy timeline that probate creates come into play. Probate proceedings are notoriously expensive, lengthy and ponderous. A typical probate process identifies all of your assets and debts, pays any taxes and fees that you owe (including estate tax), pays court fees, and distributes your property and assets to your heirs. This process usually takes at least 6 months, and can take even longer before your heirs actually receive anything that you have left for them. For this reason, and because of the sometimes-exorbitant fees that may be charged by lawyers and accountants during the process, probate has earned a nasty reputation.

Probate can also be a painstakingly public process. Because the probate process happens in court, the assets you own that go through a probate procedure become part of the public record. While this may not seem like a big deal to some, other people don't want that kind of intimate information available to the public.

Additionally, if your estate is entirely distributed via your will, the money that your family may need to cover the costs of your medical bills, funeral expenses and estate taxes will be tied up in probate, which can last up to a year or more. While immediate family members may have the option of requesting immediate cash from your assets during probate to cover immediate health care expenses, taxes, and fees, that process comes with its own set of complications. Choosing alternative methods for distributing your legacy can make life easier for your loved ones and can help them claim more of your estate in a more timely fashion than traditional methods.

A simpler and less tedious approach is to avoid probate altogether by structuring your estate to be distributed outside of the probate process. Two common ways of doing this are by structuring your assets with beneficiary designations, and creating a revocable living trust. Always consult a qualified estate-planning attorney regarding your individual situation.

Problem #2: Unintentionally Disinheriting Your Family

You would never want to unintentionally disinherit a loved one or loved ones because of confusion surrounding your legacy plan. Unfortunately, it happens. Why? This terrible situation is typically caused by a simple lack of understanding. In particular, mistakes regarding legacy distribution occur with regards to those whom people care for the most: their grandchildren.

One of the most important ways to plan for the inheritance of your grandchildren is by properly structuring the distribution of your legacy. Specifically, you need to know if your legacy is going to be distributed *per stirpes* or *per capita*.

Per Stirpes. *Per stirpes* is a legal term in Latin that means "by the branch." Your estate will be distributed *per stirpes* if you designate each branch of your family to receive an equal share of your estate. In the event that your children predecease you, their share will be distributed evenly between their children—your grandchildren.

Per Capita. *Per capita* distribution is different in that you may designate different amounts of your estate to be distributed to members of the same generation.

Per stirpes distribution of assets will follow the family tree down the line as the predecessor beneficiaries pass away. On the other hand, per capita distribution of assets ends on the branch of the family tree with the death of a designated beneficiary. For example, when your child passes away, in a per capita distribution, your grandchildren would not receive distributions from the assets that you designated to your child.

What the terms mean is not nearly as important as what they do, however. The reality is that improperly titled assets could accidentally leave your grandchildren disinherited upon the death of their parents. It's easy to check, and it's even easier to fix.

A simple way to remember the difference between the two types of distribution goes something like this: "*Stirpes are forever and Capita is capped.*"

LIFE INSURANCE: AN IMPORTANT LEGACY TOOL

One of the most powerful legacy tools you can leverage is a good life insurance policy. Life insurance is a highly efficient legacy tool because it creates money when it is needed or desired the most. Over the years, life insurance has become less expensive, while it offers more features, and it provides longer guarantees.

There are many unique benefits of life insurance that can help your beneficiaries get the most out of your legacy. Some of them include:

- Providing beneficiaries with a tax-free, liquid asset.
- Covering the costs associated with your death.
- Providing income for your dependents.
- Offering an investment opportunity for your beneficiaries.
- Covering expenses such as tuition or mortgage down payments for your children or grandchildren.

Very few people want life insurance, but nearly everyone wants what it does. Life insurance is specifically, and uniquely, capable of creating money when it is needed most. When a loved one passes, no amount of money can remove the pain of loss. And certainly, money doesn't solve the challenges that might arise with losing someone important.

It has been said that when you have money, you have options. When you don't have money, your options are severely limited. You might imagine a life insurance policy can give your family and loved ones options that would otherwise be impossible.

> » *Ed spent the last 20 years building a small business. In so many ways, it is a family business. Each of his three children, Maddie, Ruby and Owen, worked in the shop part-time during high school. But after all three attended college, only Maddie returned to join her father, and eventually will run the business full-time when Ed retires.*
>
> *Ed is able to retire comfortably on Social Security and on-going income from the shop, but the business is nearly his entire financial legacy. It is his wish that Maddie own the business outright, but he also wants to leave an equal legacy to each of his three children.*

There is no simple way to divide the business into thirds and still leave the business intact for Maddie.

Ed ends up buying a life insurance policy to make up the difference. Ruby and Owen will receive their share of an inheritance in cash from the life insurance policy and Maddie will be able to inherit the business intact.

Ed is able to accomplish his goals, treat all three children equitably and leave Maddie the business she helped to build.

If you have a life insurance policy but you haven't looked at it in a while, you may not know how it operates, how much it is worth and how it will be distributed to your beneficiaries. You may also need to update your beneficiaries on your policy. In short, without a comprehensive review of your policy, you don't really know where the money will go or to whom it will go.

If you don't have a life insurance policy but are looking for options to maintain and grow your legacy, speaking with a professional can show you the benefits of life insurance. Many people don't consider buying a life insurance policy until some event in their life triggers it, like the loss of a loved one, an accident or a health condition.

BENEFITS OF LIFE INSURANCE

Life insurance is a useful and secure tool for contingency planning, ensuring that your dependents receive the assets that you want them to have, and for meeting the financial goals you have set for the future. While it bears the name "Life Insurance," it is, in reality, a diverse financial tool that can meet many needs. The main function of a life insurance policy is to provide financial assets for your survivors. Life insurance is particularly efficient at achieving this goal because it provides a tax-advantaged lump sum of money in the form of a death benefit to your beneficiary or beneficiaries. That financial asset can be used in a number of ways. It can be structured as an investment to provide income for your spouse or children, it can pay down debts, and it can be used to cover estate taxes and other costs associated with death.

Tax liabilities on the estate you leave behind are inevitable. Capital property, for instance, is taxed at its fair market value at the time of your death, unless that property is transferred to your spouse. If the property has appreciated during the time you owned it, taxation on capital gains will occur. The unique benefits of a life insurance policy provide ways to handle this tax burden, solving any liquidity problems that may arise if your family members want to hold onto an illiquid asset, such as a piece of property or an investment. Life insurance can provide a significant amount of money to a family member or other beneficiary, and that money is likely to remain exempt from taxation or seizure.

One of life insurance's most important benefits is that it is not considered part of the estate of the policyholder. The death benefit that is paid by the insurance company goes exclusively to the beneficiaries listed on the policy. This shields the proceeds of the policy from fees and costs that can reduce an estate, including probate proceedings, attorneys' fees and claims made by creditors. The distribution of your life insurance policy is also unaffected by delays of the estate's distribution, like probate. Your beneficiaries will get the proceeds of the policy in a timely fashion, regardless of how long it takes for the rest of your estate to be settled.

Investing a portion of your assets in a life insurance policy can also protect that portion of your estate from creditors. If you owe money to someone or some entity at the time of your death, a creditor is not able to claim any money from a life insurance policy or an annuity, for that matter. An exception to this rule is if you had already used the life insurance policy as collateral against a loan. If a large portion of the money you want to dedicate to your legacy is sitting in a savings account, investment or other liquid form, creditors may be able to receive their claim on it before your beneficiaries get anything, that is if there's anything left. A life insurance policy protects your assets from creditors and ensures that your beneficiaries get the money that you intend them to have.

HOW MUCH LIFE INSURANCE DO YOU NEED?

Determining the type of policy and the amount right for you depends on an analysis of your needs. A financial professional can help you complete a needs analysis that will highlight the amount of insurance that you require to meet your goals. This type of personalized review will allow you to determine ways to continue providing income for your spouse or any dependents you may have. A financial professional can also help you calculate the amount of income that your policy should replace to meet the needs of your beneficiaries and the duration of the distribution of that income.

You may also want to use your life insurance policy to meet any expenses associated with your death. These can include funeral costs, fees from probate and legal proceedings, and taxes. You may also want to dedicate a portion of your policy proceeds to help fund tuition or other expenses for your children or grandchildren. You can buy a policy and hope it covers all of those costs, or you can work with a professional who can calculate exactly how much insurance you need and how to structure it to meet your goals. Which would you rather do?

AVOIDING POTENTIAL SNAGS

There are benefits to having life insurance supersede the direction given in a will or other estate plan, but there are also some potential snags that you should address to meet your wishes. For example, if your will instructs that your assets be divided equally between your two children, but your life insurance beneficiary is listed as just one of the children, the assets in the life insurance policy will only be distributed to the child listed as the beneficiary. The beneficiary designation of your life insurance supersedes your will's instruction. This is important to understand when designating beneficiaries on a policy you purchase. Work with a professional to make sure that your beneficiaries are accurately listed on your assets, especially your life insurance policies.

USING LIFE INSURANCE TO BUILD YOUR LEGACY

Depending on your goals, there are strategies you can use that could multiply how much you leave behind. Life insurance is one of the most surefire and efficient investment tools for building a substantial legacy that will meet your financial goals.

Here is a brief overview of how life insurance can boost your legacy:

- Life insurance provides an immediate increase in your legacy.
- It provides an income tax-advantaged death benefit for your beneficiaries.
- A good life insurance policy has the opportunity to accumulate value over time.
- It may have an option to include long-term care (LTC) or chronic illness benefits should you require them.

If your Green Money income needs for retirement are met and you have Yellow Money assets that will provide for your future expenses, you may have extra assets that you want to earmark as legacy funds. By electing to invest those assets into a life insurance policy, you can immediately increase the amount of your legacy. Remember, **life insurance allows you to transfer a tax-advantaged lump sum of money to your beneficiaries. It remains in your control during your lifetime, can provide for your long-term care needs and bypasses probate costs.** And make no mistake, taxes can have a huge impact on your legacy.

Not only that, income and assets from your legacy can have tax implications for your beneficiaries, as well.

Here's a brief overview of how taxes could affect your legacy and your beneficiaries:

- The higher your income, the higher the rate at which it is taxed.
- Withdrawals from qualified plans are taxed as income.
- What's more, when you leave a large qualified plan, it ends up being taxed at a high rate.
- If you left a $500,000 IRA to your child, they could end up owing as much as $140,000 in income taxes.
- However, if you could just withdraw $50,000 a year, the tax bill might only be $10,000 per year.

How could you use that annual amount to leave a larger legacy? Luckily, you can leverage a life insurance policy to avoid those tax penalties, preserving a larger amount of your legacy and freeing your beneficiaries from an added tax burden.

> » *When Margaret turned 70 years old, she decided it was time to look into life insurance policy options. She still feels young, but she remembers that her mother died in her early 70s, and she wants to plan ahead so she can pass on some of her legacy to her grandchildren just like her grandmother did for her.*
>
> *Margareta doesn't really want to think about life insurance, but she does want the security, reliability and tax-advantaged distribution that it offers. She lives modestly, and her Social Security benefit meets most of her income needs. As the beneficiary of her late husband's Certificate of Deposit (CD), she has $100,000 in an account that she has never used and doesn't anticipate ever needing since her income needs were already met.*

*After looking at several different investment options with a professional, Margaret decides that a Single Premium life insurance policy fits her needs best. She can buy the policy with a $100,000 one-time payment and she is guaranteed that it would provide more than the value of the contract to her beneficiaries. If she left the money in the CD, it would be subject to taxes. But for every dollar that she puts into the life insurance policy, her beneficiaries are guaranteed at least that dollar plus a death benefit, and all of it will be **tax-free!***

For $100,000, Margaret's particular policy offers a $170,000 death benefit distribution to her beneficiaries. By moving the $100,000 from a CD to a life insurance policy, Margaret increases her legacy by 70 percent. Not only that, she has also sheltered it from taxes, so her beneficiaries will be able to receive $1.70 for every $1.00 that she entered into the policy! While buying the policy doesn't allow her to use the money for herself, it does allow her family to benefit from her well-planned legacy.

MAKE YOUR WISHES KNOWN

Estate taxes used to be a much hotter topic in the mid-2000s when the estate tax limits and exclusions were much smaller and taxed at a higher rate than today. In 2008, estates valued at $2 million or more were taxed at 45 percent. Just two years later, the limit was raised to $5 million dollars taxed at 35 percent. The limit has continued to rise ever since. The limit applies to fewer people than before. Estate organization, however, is just as important as ever, and it affects everyone.

Ask yourself:

- Are your assets actually titled and held the way you think they are?
- Are your beneficiaries set up the way you think they should be?

- Have there been changes to your family or those you desire as beneficiaries?

There is more to your legacy beyond your property, money, investments and other assets that you leave to family members, loved ones and charities. Everyone has a legacy beyond money. You also leave behind personal items of importance, your values and beliefs, your personal and family history, and your wishes. Beyond a will and a plan for your assets, it is important that you make your wishes known to someone for the rest of your personal legacy. When it comes time for your family and loved ones to make decisions after you are gone, knowing your wishes can help them make decisions that honor you and your legacy, and give meaning to what you leave behind. Your professional can help you organize.

Think about your:
- Personal stories / recollections
- Values
- Personal items of emotional significance
- Financial assets

Do you want to make a plan to pass these things on to your family?

WORKING WITH A PROFESSIONAL

Part of using life insurance to your greatest advantage is selecting the policy and provider that can best meet your goals. Venturing into the jungle of policies, brokers and salespeople can be overwhelming, and can leave you wondering if you've made the best decision. Working with a trusted financial professional can help you cut through the red tape, the "sales-speak" and confusion to find a policy that meets your goals and best serves your desires for your money. If you already have a policy, a financial professional can help you review it and become familiar with the policy's premium, the guarantees the policy affords, its performance, and its features and benefits. A financial professional can also help you make any necessary changes to the policy.

> *» When Kathryn turned 88, her daughter finally convinced her to meet with a financial professional to help her organize her assets and get her legacy in order. Although Kathryn is reluctant to let a stranger in on her personal finances, she ends up very glad that she did.*
>
> *In the process of listing Kathryn's assets and her beneficiaries, her professional finds a man's name listed as the beneficiary of an old annuity that she owns. It turns out, the man is Kathryn's ex-husband who is still alive. Had Kathryn passed away before her ex-husband, the annuity and any death benefit that came from it, would have been passed on to her ex-husband. This does not reflect her latest wishes.*

Things change, relationships evolve and the way you would like your legacy organized needs to adapt to the changes that happen throughout your life. There may be a new child or grandchild in your family, or you may have been divorced or remarried. A professional will regularly review your legacy assets and ask you questions to make sure that everything is up to date and that the current organization reflects your current wishes.

CHAPTER 14 RECAP //

- To prepare for your end-of-game play, remember that beneficiary forms on policies such as your IRA and life insurance take precedence over last will and testament, trust, and divorce decree.

- Organizing your estate will ensure your wishes are properly carried through so you can effectively control your estate from the grave. Working with a financial professional can help avoid the ponderous and expensive probate process. Your professional can also make sure that you aren't unintentionally disinheriting your heirs.

- To avoid unintentional disinheritance, understand the difference between the designations *per stirpes* and *per capita*.

- Life insurance provides for the distribution of tax-free, liquid assets to your beneficiaries and can significantly build your legacy. They can also provide Living Benefits to help you pay for the high costs of medical care while you are still living.

- Working with a financial professional can help you select the policy that best meets your needs, or can help you fine tune your existing policy to better reflect your desires and intentions.

15

CHOOSING YOUR RETIREMENT COACH

From the moment you dip your toes into the retirement planning pool, to the point you start swimming laps, your assets organized, your income needs met, and your accumulation and legacy plans in place, working with a professional that you trust can make all the difference in how well your retirement reflects your desires.

It is important to know what you are looking for before taking the plunge. There are many people that would love to handle your money, but not everyone is qualified to handle it in a way that leads to a holistic approach to creating a solid retirement plan.

The distinction being made here is that you should look for someone that puts your interests first and actively wants to help you meet your goals and objectives. Oftentimes, the products someone sells you matter less than their dedication to making sure that you have a plan that meets your needs.

Professionals take your whole financial position into consideration. They make plans that adjust your risk exposure, invest in tools that secure your desired income during retirement and create investment strategies that allow you to continue accumulating wealth during your retirement for you to use later or to contribute to your legacy. If you buy stocks with a broker, use a different agent for a life insurance policy and have an unmanaged 401(k) through your employer, working with a financial professional will consolidate the management of your assets so you have one trustworthy person quarterbacking all of the team elements of your portfolio. Financial products and investment tools change, but the concepts that lie behind wise retirement planning are lasting. In the end, a financial professional's approach is designed for those serious about planning for retirement. *Can you say the same thing about the person that advises you about your financial life?*

It's easy to see how choosing a financial professional can be one of the most important decisions you can make in your life. Not only do they provide you with advice, they also manage the personal assets that supply your retirement income and contribute to your legacy. So, how do you find a good one?

HOW TO FIND A FINANCIAL PROFESSIONAL YOU CAN TRUST

Taking care to select a financial professional is one of the best things you can do for yourself and for your future. Your professional has influence and control of your investment decisions, making their role in your life more than just important. Your financial security and the quality of your retirement depends on the decisions, investment strategies and asset structuring that you and your professional create.

Working with a professional is different than calling up a broker when you want to buy or trade some stock. This isn't a decision that you can hand off to anyone else. You need to bring your time and attention to the table when it comes to finding someone with whom you can entrust your financial life. Separating the wheat from the chaff will take some work, but you'll be happy you did it.

While no one can tell you exactly who to choose or how to choose them, the following information can help you narrow the field:

- You can start by asking your friends, family and colleagues for referrals. You will want to pay particular attention to the recommendations that you get from others who are in your similar financial situation and who have similar lifestyle choices. The professional for the CEO of your company may have a different skill-set than the skill-set of the professional befitting your cousin who has 3 kids and a Subaru like you. Do follow-up research on the Internet as well, checking with your state's securities department and department of insurance. You may wish to investigate the financial professional through your local Better Business Bureau or the National Ethics Association.

- The other side of the coin, however, is that everyone and their brother has a recommendation about how you should manage your money and who should manage it for you. From hot stock tips to "the best money manager in the state," people love to share good information that makes them look like they are in the know. Nobody wants to talk about the bad stock purchases they made, the times they lost money and the poor selections they made regarding financial professionals or stock brokers. If you decide to take a friend or family member's recommendation, make sure they have a substantial, long-term experience with the financial professional and that their glowing review isn't just based on a one-time "win."

- It is important to understand how your professional is being paid. It is generally considered preferable to work with a fee-based professional who will not have conflicts of interest between earning a commission and acting in your best interests.

- Many professionals may also be brokers or dealers that can earn commissions on things like life insurance, certain types of annuities and disability insurance. These professionals have most likely intentionally overlapped their roles so that if their clients choose to purchase insurance or investment products that require a broker or dealer, those clients won't have to find an additional person to work with. Again, understanding the role of your professional will help you make your determination.

NARROWING THE FIELD

1. Decide on the Type of Professional with Whom You Want to Work. There are four basic kinds of financial professionals. Many professionals may play overlapping roles. It is important to know a professional's primary function, how they charge for their services and whether they are obligated to act in your best interest.

Registered representatives, better known as stockbrokers or bank / investment representatives, make their living by earning commissions on insurance products and investment services. Stockbrokers basically sell you things. The products from which they make the highest commission are sometimes the products that they recommend to their clients. If you want to make a simple transaction, such as buying or selling a particular stock, a registered representative can help you. Although registered representatives are licensed professionals, if you want to create a structured and planful approach to positioning your assets for retirement, you might want to consider continuing your search.

The term "planner" is often misused. It can refer to credible professionals that are CPAs, CFPs and ChFCs, to your uncle's next door neighbor who claims to have a lead on some undervalued stock about to be "discovered." A wide array of people may claim to be planners because there are no requirements to be a planner. The term financial planner, however, refers to someone who is properly registered as an investment advisor and serves as a fiduciary as described below.

Financial professionals are the diamonds in the rough. These Registered Investment Advisors are compensated on a fee basis. They do, however, often have licensure as stockbrokers or insurance agents, allowing them to earn commissions on certain transactions. More importantly, **financial professionals are financial fiduciaries, meaning they are required to make financial decisions in your best interest and reflecting your risk tolerance.** Investment Advisors are held to high ethical standards and are highly regarded in the financial industry. Financial professionals also often take a more comprehensive approach to asset management. These professionals are trained and credentialed to plan and coordinate their clients' assets in order to meet their goals or retirement and legacy planning. They are not focused on individual stocks, investments or markets. They look at the big picture, the whole enchilada.

Money managers are on par with financial professionals. However, they are often given explicit permission to make investment decisions without advanced approval by their clients.

Understanding who you are working with and what their title is the first step to planning your retirement. While each of the above-mentioned types of financial professionals can help you with aspects of your finances, it is **financial professionals** who have the most intimate role, the most objective investment strategies and the most unbiased mode of compensation for their services. A financial professional can also help you with the non-financial aspects of your legacy and can help you find ways to create a tax planning strategy to help you save money.

2. Be Objective. At the end of the day, you need to separate the weak from the strong. While you might want a strong personal rapport with your professional, or you may want to choose your professional for their personality and positive attitude, it is more important that you find someone who will give sage advice regarding achieving your retirement goals.

It can be helpful to use a process of elimination to narrow the field of potential professionals. Look into five or six potential leads and cross off your list the ones that don't meet your requirements until only one or two remain. Cross-check your remaining choices against the list of things you need from a professional. Make sure they represent a firm that has the investment tools and products that you desire, and make sure they have experience in retirement planning. That is, after all, the main goal.

Don't be afraid to investigate each of your candidates. You'll want to ask the same questions and look for the same information from everyone you consider so you can then compare them and discern which is best for you. You'll want to take a look at the specific credentials of each professional, their experience and competence, their ethics and fiduciary status, their history and track record, and a list of the services that they offer. The professionals who meet all or most of your qualifications are the ones you will contact for an interview.

Potential professionals should meet your qualifications in the following categories:

- *Credentials:* Look at their experience, the quality of their education, any associations to which they belong and certifications they have earned. Someone who has continued their professional education through ongoing certifications will be more up-to-date on current financial practices compared to someone who got their degree 25 years ago and hasn't done a thing since.

- *Practices:* Look at the track record of your candidates, how they are compensated for their services, the reports and analysis they offer, and their value added services.
- *Services:* Your professional must meet your needs. If you are planning your retirement, you should work with someone who offers services that help you to that end. You want someone who can offer planning, advice on investment strategies, ways to calculate risk, advice on insurance and annuities products, and ways to manage your tax strategy.
- *Ethics:* You want to work with someone who is above board and does things the right way. Vet them by checking their compliance record, current licensing, fiduciary status and, yes, even their criminal record. You never know!

3. Use the Internet. As a final step before picking up the phone and calling your candidates, do some digging to discover if anyone on your list has a history of unlawful or unethical practices, or has been disciplined for any of their professional behavior or decisions. Don't worry, you don't have to hire a private investigator. You can easily find this information on the Financial Industry Regulatory Authority's (FINRA) online BrokerCheck tool: http://www.finra.org/Investors/ToolsCalculators/BrokerCheck/.

You should obviously explore the website of a potential professional and the website of the firm that they represent. The Internet allows you to go beyond the online business card of a professional to gain access to information that they don't control. It may all be good information! Or a brief search of the Internet could reveal a sketchy past. The best part is that the Internet allows you to find helpful information in an anonymous fashion.

Start with Google (www.google.com) and search the name of a potential professional and their firm. Keep your eyes trained on third party sources such as articles, blog posts or news stories that mention the professional. You can also check a professional's compliance records online with the Financial Industry Regulatory Authority (FINRA) and the Securities and Exchange Commission (SEC). If you want to dig deeper, you can combine search terms like "scams," "lawsuits," "suspensions" and "fraud" with a professional's or firm's name to see what information arises. More likely than not, you won't find anything. But if you do, you'll be glad that you checked.

HOW TO INTERVIEW CANDIDATES

After vetting your candidates and narrowing down a list of professionals that you think might be a good fit for you, it's time to start interviewing. Here are some possible questions you may want to ask each financial professional.

1. How do you charge for your services? How much do you charge? This information should be easy to find on their website, but if you don't see it, ask. Find out if they charge an initial planning fee, if they charge a percentage for assets under their management and if they make money by selling specific financial products or services. If so, you should follow up by asking how much the service costs. This will give you an idea of how they really make their money and if they have incentive to sell certain products over others. Make sure you understand exactly how you will be charged so there are no surprises down the road if you decide to work with this person.

2. What are your credentials, licenses, and certifications? There are Certified Financial Planners (CFPs), Chartered Financial Consultants (ChFCs), Investment Advisor Representatives, Certified Public Accountants (CPAs) and Personal Financial Specialists (PFSs). Whatever their credentials or titles, you want to be sure that the professional you work with is an expert in the field relevant to your circumstances. If you want someone to manage your money, you will most likely look for an Investment Advisor. Someone that works with an independent firm will likely have a team of CPAs, CFPs and other financial experts upon whom they can draw. If you like the professional you are meeting with and you think they might be a good fit, but they don't have the accounting experience you want them to have, ask about their firm and the resources available to them. If they work closely with CPAs that are experienced in your needs, it could be a good match.

3. What are the financial services that you and your firm provide? The question within the question here is, "Can you help me achieve my goals?" Some people can only provide you with investment advice, and others are tax consultants. You will likely want to work with someone that provides a complete suite of financial planning services and products that touch on retirement planning, insurance options, legacy and estate structuring, and tax planning. Whatever services they provide, make sure they meet your needs and your anticipated needs.

4. What kinds of clients do you work with the most? A lot of financial professionals work within a niche: retirement planning, risk assessment, life insurance, etc. Finding someone who works with other people that are in the same financial boat as you and who have similar goals can be an important way to make sure they understand your needs. While someone might be a crackerjack annuities cowboy, you might not be interested in that option. Ask follow-up questions that will really help you understand where their expertise lies and whether or not their experience lines up with your needs.

5. May I see a sample of one of your financial plans? You wouldn't buy a car without test driving it, and you should not work with a professional without seeing a sample of how they do business. While there is no formal structure that a financial plan has to follow, the variation between professionals can help you find someone who "speaks your language." One professional may provide you with an in-depth analysis that relies heavily on info graphics and diagrams. Someone else may give you a seven-page review of your assets and general recommendations. By seeing a sample plan, you can narrow down who presents information in the way that you desire and in ways that you understand.

6. How do you approach investing? You may be entirely in the dark about how to approach your investments, or you might have some guiding principles. Either way, ask each candidate what their philosophy is. Some will resonate with you and some won't. A good professional who has a realistic approach to investing won't promise you the moon or tell you that they can make you a lot of money. Professionals who are successful at retirement planning and full service financial management will tell you that they will listen to your goals, risk tolerance and comfort level with different types of investment strategies. Working with someone that you trust is critical, and this question in particular can help you find out who you can and who you can't.

7. How do you remain in contact with your clients? Does your prospective professional hold annual, quarterly or monthly meetings? How often do *you* want to meet with your professional? Some people want to check in once a year, go over everything and make sure their ducks are all in a row. If any changes over the previous year or additions to their legacy planning strategy came up, they'll do it on that date. Other people want a monthly update to be more involved in the decision making process and to understand what's happening with their portfolio. You basically need to determine the right degree of involvement for both you and your financial professional. You'll also want to feel out how your professional communicates. Do you prefer phone calls or face-to-face meetings? Do you want your professional to explain things to you in detail or to summarize for you what decisions they've made?

8. Are you my main contact, or do you work with a team? This is another way of finding out how involved with you your professional will be, and how often they will meet with you. It is also a way to discover how the firm they represent operates and manages their clients. Some professionals will answer their own phone, meet with you regularly and have your home phone number on speed dial. Others will meet with you once a year and have a partner or assistant check in with you every quarter to give you an update. Other companies take an entirely team-based approach whereby clients have a main contact but their portfolio is handled by a team of professionals that represent the firm. One way isn't better than another, but one way will be best for you. Find out how the professional you are interviewing operates before entering into an agreement.

9. Did they ask questions and show signs that they were interested in working with me? A professional who will structure your assets to reflect your risk tolerance and to position you for a comfortable retirement must be a good listener. You will want to pass by a professional who talks non-stop and tells you what to do without listening to what you want them to do. If you felt they listened well and understood your needs, and seemed interested and experienced in your situation, then they might be right for you.

THE IMPORTANCE OF INDEPENDENCE

Not all investment firms and financial professionals are created equal. The information in this book has systematically shown that leveraging investments for income and accumulation in today's market requires new ideas and modern planning. In short, you need innovative ideas to come up with the creative solutions that will provide you with the retirement that you want. Innovation thrives on independence. No matter how good a financial professional is, the firm that they represent needs to operate on principles that make sense in today's economy. Remember, advice about money has been around forever. Good advice, however, changes with the times.

Timing the market, relying on the sale of stocks for income and banking on high treasury and bond returns are not strategies. They aren't even realistic ways to make money or to generate income. Working with an independent advisor can help you break free from the old ways of thinking and position you to create a realistic retirement plan.

Working with an independent professional who relies on fee-based income tied to the success of their performance will also give you greater peace of mind. When you do well, they do well, and that's the way it should be. Your independent financial professional will make sure that:

- Your assets are organized and structured to reflect your risk tolerance.
- Your assets will be available to you when you need them and in the way that you need them.
- You will have a lifetime income that will support your lifestyle through your retirement.
- You are handling your taxes as efficiently as possible.
- Your legacy is in order.
- Your Red Money is turned into Yellow Money, and is managed in your best interest.

» *Remember Raymond and Diane from Chapter 1? Even though they knew they had Social Security benefits coming, they placed some money in savings and each had a pension or a 401(k). Before they met with a financial professional, they had no idea what their retirement would look like. After they met with an advisor, they knew exactly what types of assets they had, how much they were worth, how much risk they were exposed to and how they were going to be distributed. They also created an income plan so that they could pay their bills every month the moment they retired, and they maximized their Social Security benefit by targeting the year and month they would get the most lifetime benefits. After their income needs were met, they were able to continue accumulating wealth by investing their extra assets to serve them in the future and contribute to their legacy. Their professional also helped them make decisions that impacted their taxes, protecting the value of their assets and allowing them to keep more of their money.*

This isn't a fairy tale scenario. This is an example of how much you stand to gain by meeting with a financial professional who can help you create a planful approach to your retirement. The concept of Know So and Hope So didn't just apply to their money, it also applied to Raymond and Diane. They hoped that they would have enough for retirement and that they had worked hard enough and saved enough to maintain their lifestyle. Working with a financial professional allowed them to know that their income needs were secured and structured to provide them with income for the rest of their lives and with some money to spare.

Now, ask yourself: Is your retirement built on hopes and dreams, or a solid, predictable plan?

IT'S WORTH IT!

Finding, interviewing and selecting a financial professional can seem like a daunting task. And honestly, it will take a good amount of work to narrow the field and find the one you want. In the end, it is worth the blood, sweat and tears. Your retirement, lifestyle, assets and legacy is on the line. The choices you make today will have lasting impacts on your life and the life of your loved ones. Working with someone you trust and know you can rely on to make decisions that will benefit you is invaluable. The work it takes to find them is something you will never regret.

Here is a recap of why working with a financial professional is the best retirement decision you can make:

CHAPTER 15 RECAP //

- Look for professionals held to fiduciary standards of liability who put your interests first and actively want to help you meet your goals and objectives. Your risk tolerance, needs, wants, liquidity concerns and timeline worries should be the focus of the meeting before they try to sell you any products.
- To find a professional you can trust, start by asking family and friends for referrals. Make sure to do your due diligence and check out anyone who is recommended to you.
- When interviewing candidates, ask questions such as, "How often do you check in with your clients?" "May I see a sample of one of your financial plans?" And, "How do you approach investing?" These questions will help ensure that you and your professional are a good fit for each other.
- Not all investment firms and financial professionals are created equal. Working with an independent professional will give you more options that are customizable to your life.